OECD
ECONOMIC SURVEYS

AUSTRIA

ORGANISATION FOR ECONOMIC CO-OPERATION AND DEVELOPMENT

Pursuant to article 1 of the Convention signed in Paris on 14th December 1960, and which came into force on 30th September 1961, the Organisation for Economic Co-operation and Development (OECD) shall promote policies designed:

- to achieve the highest sustainable economic growth and employment and a rising standard of living in Member countries, while maintaining financial stability, and thus to contribute to the development of the world economy;
- to contribute to sound economic expansion in Member as well as non-member countries in the process of economic development; and
- to contribute to the expansion of world trade on a multilateral, non-discriminatory basis in accordance with international obligations.

The original Member countries of the OECD are Austria, Belgium, Canada, Denmark, France, the Federal Republic of Germany, Greece, Iceland, Ireland, Italy, Luxembourg, the Netherlands, Norway, Portugal, Spain, Sweden, Switzerland, Turkey, the United Kingdom and the United States. The following countries became Members subsequently through accession at the dates indicated hereafter: Japan (28th April 1964), Finland (28th January 1969), Australia (7th June 1971) and New Zealand (29th May 1973).

The Socialist Federal Republic of Yugoslavia takes part in some of the work of the OECD (agreement of 28th October 1961).

Publié également en français.

Contents

Tables

Diagrams

This Survey is based on the Secretariat's study prepared for the annual review of Austria by the Economic and Development Review Committee on 17th January 1989.

•

After revisions in the light of discussions during the review, final approval of the Survey for publication was given by the Committee on 14th February 1989.

•

The previous survey of Austria was issued in February 1988.

BASIC STATISTICS OF AUSTRIA

THE LAND

Area (thousand km²)	84	Major cities, 1981 census (thousands of inhabitants):	
Agricultural area (thousand km²), 1988	33	Vienna	1 531
Exploited forest area (thousand km²)	32	Graz	243
		Linz	200
		Salzburg	139
		Innsbruck	117

THE PEOPLE

Population, 01.01.87 (thousands)	7 570	Net migration, 1987	15 000
per km²	90	Total employment[1], monthly average 1987	2 785 359
Net natural increase in population, 1987	2 000	*of which:*	
Natural increase rate per 1 000 inhabitants, 1987	0.3	in industry[2]	543 605

PRODUCTION

Gross Domestic Product, 1987 (Sch. billion)	1 482	Industrial origin of GDP at market prices, 1987 (per cent):	
per head (US $)	15 478	Agriculture	3
Gross fixed investment 1987:		Industry	27
per cent of GDP	23	Construction	7
per head (US $)	3 489	Other	63

THE GOVERNMENT

Public consumption, 1987 (per cent of GDP)	19	Composition of Federal Parliament:	
General government current revenue, 1987		Socialist Party	90
(per cent of GDP)	47	Austrian People's Party	77
Federal Government debt, end 1987 (per cent of GDP) 47.0		Liberal Party	18
		Greens	8
		Last election: November 1986	

FOREIGN TRADE

Exports:		Imports:	
Exports of goods and services 1987		Imports of goods and services, 1987	
(per cent of GDP)	36	(per cent of GDP)	35
Exports, 1987 (per cent of total merchandise exports):		Imports, 1987 (per cent of total merchandise imports):	
Food, tobacco, beverages	3	Food, tobacco, beverages	6
Raw materials and energy	7	Raw materials and energy	12
Chemicals	9	Chemicals	10
Machinery and transport equipment	33	Machinery and transport equipment	35
Other finished and semi-manufactured products	47	Other finished and semi-manufactured products	37

THE CURRENCY

Monetary unit: Schilling		Currency units per US dollar, average of daily figures:	
		Year 1988	12.34
		January 1989	12.87

1. Wage and salary earners.
2. Including administrative personnel.
Note: An international comparison of certain basic statistics is given in an annex table.

Introduction

Austria's economic performance has improved appreciably since mid-1987. The flagging economic expansion has picked up sharply, helped by a much-improved international environment. In 1988 output grew by about 4 per cent, somewhat faster than the European average. Inflation, though edging up, remained low by Austrian and international standards and the rise in unemployment has been reversed. The favourable business situation has set the stage for continued expansion over the coming two years, though this is likely to be at a slower pace than in 1988. Exports can be expected to remain the mainstay of growth and domestic-demand expansion should be backed-up by a further lowering of the saving ratio. Moderate wage settlements should keep inflation low. This in conjunction with continued buoyancy of export markets could make for some strengthening of the current external account position.

The Government's medium-term financial programme has dominated economic policy making since 1987. The federal budget deficit was reduced in 1987 and 1988 in line with stated objectives, but despite a faster-than-expected expansion of the economy, the 1989 outlook is for a slowing of the consolidation process. However, looking beyond the next few years the public sector's financial position should no longer be weakened by net revenue losses entailed by the 1989 tax reform; indeed, over the medium to longer run this might even be revenue-raising, because of positive supply-side effects. Moreover, the restructuring of nationalised industries has already produced some positive results whose impact on the federal budget will, however, only be felt gradually over the next decade.

Part I of this Survey reviews the first years of budget consolidation, recent developments of monetary policy and the progress made on improving the supply side of the economy. Against this policy background, salient features of economic developments in 1988 and the projections for 1989 and 1990 are discussed in Part II. Part III returns to issues pertaining to the medium-term fiscal programme taking as a starting point the major factors behind the trend rise in public expenditure and weak revenue growth. The principal measures taken, and options being considered, to reverse these trends are examined, including the 1989 tax reform and a brief review of the continuing debate on the reform of the social security system. The main findings of the Survey and some policy considerations are presented in the Conclusions.

I. Economic policies: a mid-term review

Main features of the economic strategy

The present Government took office two years ago. It has a large majority in Parliament, facilitating the handling of difficult economic and social issues. A key element of the coalition agreement was the establishment of a comprehensive economic reform programme. Its principal aim was to improve the performance of the economy, which had shown a conspicuous trend decline since the beginning of the 1980s (OECD 1988a):

- Average economic growth from 1980 to 1986 was somewhat below the already weak European average (1.5 per cent versus 1.9 per cent per annum) and unemployment, though remaining low by international comparison, steadily increased over the same period, from 2.1 per cent to 3.7 per cent;
- The traditional "flagships" of the Austrian economy – the nationalised industries – were recording increasingly large losses, indicating structural weakness;
- The federal budget deficit almost doubled in relation to GDP from 2.6 per cent in 1981 to 5.1 per cent in 1986, entailing a rapid rise in debt-interest payments.

While maintaining traditional elements of previous governments' policy approach, notably the hard-currency option and social partnership, the Government embarked upon two new policy avenues: adoption of a medium-term fiscal policy framework and improvement of the economy's supply responsiveness in face of increasing international competition.

The re-orientation of *fiscal policy* away from its traditional role of demand management and employment support, was prompted by several events and considerations. First, less than half of the post-OPEC II widening of the budget deficit was recuperated in the subsequent, weakish, recovery. Secondly, based on unchanged expenditure and tax policies, the budget outlook in 1987 five years ahead pointed to a continued worsening of the deficit, a soaring debt burden, and interest payments increasingly crowding out other government expenditure. Thirdly, given much more favourable trends of public finance in Germany, the hard-currency option was seen to be put at risk. Against this background, a *medium-term framework* for fiscal policy has been adopted, aiming at stabilising the debt/GDP ratio by 1992. Starting from an earlier-projected 1987 budget deficit of 5½ per cent of GDP and assuming a fairly modest average nominal income growth (4½ per cent per year) as well as unchanged nominal interest rates, an average annual reduction of the federal budget deficit/GDP ratio by half a percentage point was required to bring the deficit down to 2½ per cent of GDP by 1992.

The initial focus of the new Government's *supply-side policies* was the revitalisation of loss-making nationalised industries. This has involved the restructuring of various companies and cuts in the workforce. Furthermore, there have been, and will be, further reductions in the federal share in several state-owned firms, along with privatisation of some companies. Positive supply-side effects were also expected to result from reforms in the field of taxation. Apart from increasing the responsiveness of tax revenue to GDP growth, the reform programme is to encourage risk-taking and to strengthen incentives to invest and work, by lowering marginal tax rates and removing distortions. Market access is to be facilitated by an easing of regulation on firms, notably small and medium-sized enterprises. Finally, measures were envisaged to accelerate diffusion of new technologies and, more generally, to speed up "modernisation" of industry.

Fiscal policy: towards budget consolidation

Budget consolidation in the 1980s started later than in many other Member countries. Even so, moves towards a more balanced budget position are being taken in small steps, reversing, however, what had become a rapidly deteriorating trend (Diagram 1). In the initial 1987 consolidation programme, the federal budget deficit was to be reduced in the three years to 1989 by Sch. 9 billion to Sch. 66 billion. Given that the final outcome of the 1987 budget was more favourable than anticipated, the cumulative deficit reduction in 1988 and 1989 is likely to be only half of the amount originally planned.

12

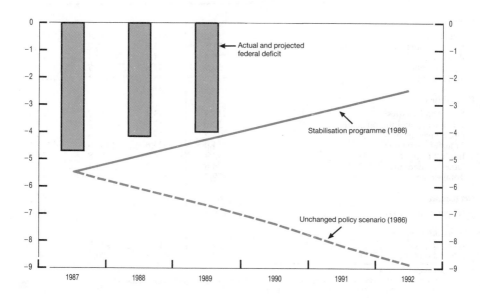

Diagram 1.   **BUDGET CONSOLIDATION AND
THE MEDIUM-TERM STRATEGY**
(Per cent of GDP)

Actual and projected federal deficit

Stabilisation programme (1986)

Unchanged policy scenario (1986)

Sources: Federal Press Service (1987) and OECD.

1987 Federal budget: conflicting short- and medium-term concerns

In 1987, fiscal policy was caught in a dilemma between the short-run objective of supporting the faltering economic expansion and the medium-term requirement to rein in the deficit. Consequently, expenditure restraint was mainly applied to financial transactions, i.e. budgetary items with small or no direct effects on demand. Moreover, to reach the targeted financial balance, additional asset sales were undertaken and tax expenditures were reduced by bringing forward the expiration of the investment premium and reducing savings promotion. The outcome for 1987 was a *budget deficit* (net of debt repayments) of Sch. 69.8 billion (Table 1). This was about Sch. 3 billion less than the year before and almost Sch. 5 billion less than envisaged in the medium-term programme. Measured in relation to GDP, the deficit came to 4.7 per cent compared to 5.1 per cent in 1986.

13

Table 1.   **The Federal Budget, 1987-1989**

Administrative basis, schilling billion

	1987	1988 Budget	1988[1] Outturn	1989 Budget
Revenue				
Net taxes[2]	280.8	311.5	317.1	323.2
Income from federal enterprises	71.5	77.5	76.7	79.8
Asset sales	6.4	4.7	3.4	12.0
Other revenue	50.9	52.8	53.7	50.4
Total revenue	409.6	446.5	451.1	465.4
Expenditure				
Wages and salaries[3]	113.9	113.4	115.7	117.8
Current expenditure on goods	52.0	55.6	56.2	57.1
Gross investment	24.5	25.8	26.8	26.1
Transfer payments	214.0	239.6	237.9	252.3
Interest payments	48.4	54.0	51.8	55.0
Other expenditure	26.6	29.2	29.1	23.2
Total expenditure	479.4	517.6	517.5	531.5
Net balance	–69.8	–71.1	–66.4	–66.1
(In per cent of GDP)	(–4.7)	(–4.6)	(–4.2)	(–4.0)
Memorandum items :				
Revenue, net[4]	409.2	419.3	424.9	438.6
Expenditure, net[4]	479.3	495.8	490.0	513.4

1. As of December 1988.
2. Total tax revenue less tax sharing plus tax-like revenue (mainly social security contributions).
3. Including salaries to teachers employed by the States.
4. Net of double accounting and reserve operations on a cash basis.
Sources :   Ministry of Finance, *Bundesfinanzgesetz 1988* and *Bundesvoranschlag 1989*.

The deficit reduction was achieved despite sluggish *revenue* increases. Indeed, amounting to 4.6 per cent, the growth of receipts was the lowest since 1982. Tax receipts were depressed by slow growth of wages and salaries, the disinflationary impact of lower oil prices and more generous household income tax allowances. With stagnating employment, the rise in social security contributions was also moderate. On the other hand, as noted above, budget revenues were bolstered by augmented *asset sales*, amounting to Sch. 6½ billion. Total *disbursements* advanced even less rapidly than revenues, mainly because cyclical influences on automatic budget stabilisers were weaker than initially expected. On the other hand, there was continued upward momentum in pension outlays and interest payments. Transfers to the pension insurance scheme rose because of demographic developments, notably longer life expectancy, but also because of an increased tendency towards early retirement in the face of excess labour supply. The early retirement scheme allows male workers to receive a pension at the age of 60 and female workers at 55. Despite lower interest rates, interest payments continued to drift upwards, accounting for 10 per cent of total disbursements and absorbing 22 per cent of taxes after revenue sharing.

The 1988 Federal budget: benefiting from conjunctural gains

The 1988 Federal Budget was the first to reflect the full impact of the Government's medium-term budget consolidation efforts. In addition, the financial position was strengthened by automatic stabilisers. Despite smaller-than-budgeted asset sales, the actual deficit may turn out some Sch. 4¾ billion lower than originally planned. The faster-than-anticipated rise in tax receipts and savings on unemployment benefits, taken together, may have improved the balance by some Sch. 9 billion. However, since more than half – Sch. 6 billion – of this conjunctural gain is going to be transferred to the Labour Market Fund and to reserves for planned future expenditure, the actual deficit, as shown in the final administrative account, may be about to Sch. 66 billion, or 4.2 per cent of GDP, against 4.7 per cent in 1987.

According to preliminary estimates, total *federal expenditure*, including the above-mentioned additions to reserves, remained flat, against the budgeted 2¼ per cent rate of growth. As a result, the federal expenditure/GDP ratio fell sharply from 35 per cent in 1987 to 33 per cent. Budget economies were made in a broad range of spending categories, with particular efforts being directed towards limiting the growth of the public sector wage bill. New vacancies were only partially filled, appropriations for overtime payments were cut and a six-month delay in wage adjustments for civil servants was imposed. Lower transfers and subsidies to the Länder (for residential construction), the federal railways, agriculture, as well as to industry and trade helped to check expenditure growth. The Government also took first steps to limit the upward drift of transfers to households, curtailing family welfare benefits such as marriage and education allowances (see Annex I, Calendar of Main Economic Events). Due to better labour-market conditions, transfers to the unemployment funds and to the social insurance system grew less than budgeted. Interest payments continued to rise, though at a more moderate pace and less than budgeted, reflecting rescheduling from higher to lower interest-bearing debt. Transfers to the Austrian State Holding Company (ÖIAG), however, increased as a result of past commitments (see below), notwithstanding a sharp reduction in balance sheet losses (from Sch. 8 billion in 1987 to just under Sch. 3 billion in 1988). While *federal revenues*, boosted by stronger economic activity, grew faster than budgeted (3½ per cent compared to 2¼ per cent), the aggregate federal tax burden remained

15

virtually unchanged at around 29 per cent of GDP. Both wage and value-added tax proceeds have grown more strongly than envisaged in the initial budget, more than compensating for lower-than-budgeted revenues from asset sales.

The 1989 Federal budget: little further progress in budget consolidation

In the recently voted Budget for 1989, the deficit is brought further down to 4 per cent of GDP, consistent with the Medium-term Plan. However, adjusting for the build-up of extra reserves in 1988 and fluctuations in asset sales, the underlying budget position shows renewed weakening. In assessing the 1989 budget proposal, it should be noted, though, that the 1989 Tax Reform entails gross tax reductions to the tune of Sch. 45 billion or 50 per cent more than envisaged in the initial working agreement between the coalition parties, and that initial claims for resources by individual ministries would have led to a deficit of Sch. 96 billion. The first-year revenue shortfall directly associated with the tax reform is estimated at Sch. 10 billion, of which about half will be carried by the Federal government (including the reduction of fiscal drag). Proceeds from asset sales are expected to yield Sch. 12 billion, of which Sch. 8 billion from selling the Mint to the National Bank. Disbursements are projected to grow by 2¾ per cent. By contrast, transfer payments are expected to rise strongly, mainly attributable to an increase in the federal contribution to the pension system.

Summing up, the change in the federal government deficit over the three years to 1989 will probably be closely in line with the medium-term plan. However, the budget consolidation process has benefited significantly from asset sales, raising net Sch. 19 billion, and from the stronger-than-expected growth of the economy. The counterpart has been an only moderately less demand-supportive fiscal stance. Indeed, according to a measure of the stance of fiscal policy used by the Austrian Institute for Economic Research (WIFO), and based on preliminary data for 1988, the tightening of fiscal policy was very moderate in 1988 and may not continue in 1989. Weighting expenditure and revenue components by their respective multipliers, the "demand-effective" deficit was reduced to 4½ per cent in 1988, and is estimated to increase to 5 per cent in 1989.

Federal government expenditure accounts for about half of general government outlays. Local governments (Länder and municipalities) contribute most to public consumption and investment, while the larger part of transfers is financed by the federal government and social security funds. Local government budgets have traditionally been in deficit on an administrative basis, but on a national accounts

Table 2. **The stance of fiscal policy**

Per cent of GDP

	1987	1988	1989
Change in general government net lending	−0.5	1.4	−¼
of which :			
Due to automatic stabilizers[1]	−0.1	1.2	½
Change in structural balance[2]	−0.4	0.2	−¾

1. Automatic stabilizers represent the cyclical component of the budget balance, estimated as the reaction of the budget to differences between real GDP growth and its trend rate.
2. A positive sign indicates a move towards restriction (surplus), while a negative sign indicates expansion, i.e. public expenditure increases and/or tax reductions. The measure reflects, apart from deliberate policy actions, aslo fiscal drag and changes in debt service cost.
Sources : OECD, estimates and projections.

basis i.e. without lending to the private sector, they usually are in surplus. The *general government financial deficit* is estimated to shrink from 4 per cent in 1987 to 2¾ per cent in 1988 and could increase again to less than 3 per cent in 1989. Changes in the budget balance can be broken down into a cyclical and a structural component. The former can be measured by the effect on the budget of deviations of GDP from its trend growth rate, while the latter, apart from discretionary policy actions, includes fiscal drag and changes in debt-service costs. As can be seen from Table 2, the deliberate move towards increasing fiscal support was reversed in 1988 but will, on present budget prospects, be resumed in 1989 when the damping demand effect of automatic stabilisers is projected to diminish.

Monetary policy: supporting the hard-currency course

Since the breakdown of the Bretton-Woods system of fixed exchange rates, the main target of monetary policy has been to stabilise the external value of the schilling. In early post-Smithsonian years, the exchange rate was related to changing currency baskets. Since the late 1970s, however, the authorities have moved towards a more straightforward and transparent policy option, pegging the schilling to the Deutschemark only. The principal reason for focusing on this currency has been the close links with the German economy. With export and import shares at about 35 per cent, Germany is Austria's largest single trading partner. German tourists provide 80 per cent of foreign currency earnings from tourism and border trade is of considerable regional importance. Moreover, with Germany being a long-standing and successful inflation fighter, a measure of discipline is being imposed on the Austrian economy, keeping inflation and inflation expectations at bay.

17

Since 1982, fluctuations in the schilling-Deutschemark exchange rate have been limited. Indeed, apart from a few speculative bouts, deviations from parity have never exceeded a ¼ of a percentage point (Diagram 2). This has meant that the National Bank, if necessary, has been withdrawing or supplying foreign exchange to the amount consistent with the desired parity, either directly through intervention or indirectly by offering favourable currency swaps to the banks. As policy-controlled interest rates are determined in relation to required net capital flows, the monetary authorities do not attempt to control money creation. They can and do influence, however, the repartition between the domestic and the foreign source component of the central bank money supply through interest rate policy. The choice of instruments is determined in the light of changes in the central bank's foreign exchange position and the causal factors influencing these changes. In case of yield-determined

Diagram 2.   **THE SCHILLING/DEUTSCHEMARK EXCHANGE RATE**
(1980 = 100)

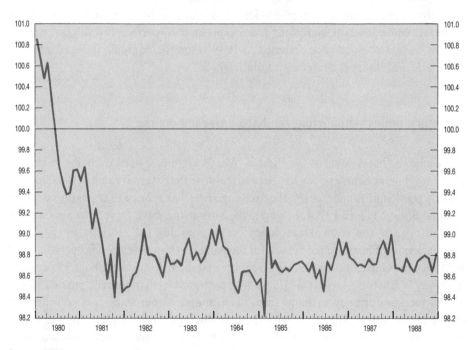

Source: OECD.

18

foreign-exchange outflows, no compensatory expansionary use of the domestic source component is made, entailing upward pressure on interest rates. Conversely, swap transactions gain importance if short-term seasonal foreign-exchange flows related to current-account transactions have to be compensated for.

Interest-rate policy and capital flows

An exchange-rate-oriented *cum* foreign-exchange-targeted policy is often said, and correctly so, to prevent the authorities from steering monetary aggregates and using interest-rate policy as an autonomous tool of demand management. In recent years, the room for pursuing an independent interest-rate policy has been further reduced by the growing internationalisation of financial markets.

In view of the relative weakness of Austria's current external-account position in recent years, and the persistent, though moderate, inflation differential *vis-à-vis* Germany, a positive premium on both short- and long-term interest rates over

Diagram 3. **POLICY ACTION AND SHORT-TERM INTEREST RATES**

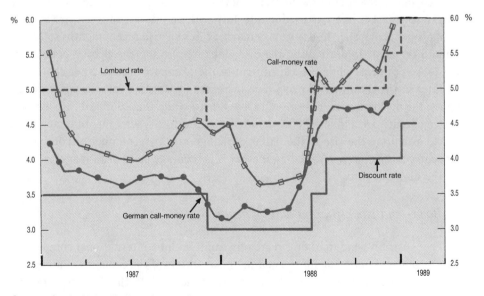

Sources: Austrian National Bank and Deutsche Bundesbank.

corresponding German rates has usually existed. Austrian money-market rates followed the decline of German short-term interest rates during 1987, apart from a short, but turbulent, period after the stock-market crash in October 1987 (Diagram 3). To fend off potential speculative pressure on the schilling exchange rate, the interest rate differential was allowed to widen to 1 percentage point. Internationally co-ordinated monetary policy actions in the wake of the stock-market crash helped to rapidly calm international financial markets, with the decline of interest rates abroad being resumed. By December 1987, the National Bank was in a position to lower its discount rate to 3 per cent and the Lombard rate to 4½ per cent.

Calmer exchange-market and international financial conditions persisted during most of the first half of 1988. Austrian money-market rates followed German rates to their nadir in late spring, with the differential slimming to ½ percentage point. This was accommodated by public sector borrowing which more than offset private net capital outflows. Net capital inflows in the first eight months of 1988 amounted to Sch. 16 billion, compared with Sch. 3.7 billion in the same period of 1987, corrected for swap transactions.

As generally elsewhere, there has been a modest tightening of monetary policy since mid-1988. In line with corresponding steps in other European hard-currency countries, the National Bank raised the interest rate for open-market operations – which have an immediate impact on the money market – in four steps to 4⅝ per cent by early August. In order to counteract a short-term tightness of the money market, a special open-market line was used in late July with an interest rate tender (bidding rate of 6⅜ per cent). Day-to-day money market rates have in recent months settled at around 5 per cent. In early July, the discount rate was increased by ½ percentage point to 3½ per cent, while the adjustment of the Lombard rate to 5 per cent came only later in the month. Following new increases in German interest rates in late August, the discount rate was raised to 4 per cent, while the Lombard rate was left unchanged until December 1988, when it increased to 5½ per cent. In a concerted move to attenuate the rise in the dollar exchange rate by a number of continental European countries, it was raised by another ½ percentage point in January, together with the discount rate.

Bond- and stock-market developments

The Austrian bond market is relatively small both by international comparison and as a source of financing for the non-financial sectors of the economy. Enterprises as well as households rely heavily on bank finance, while the Government and financial institutions play a dominant role as capital market borrowers. In 1987, the total recourse to the bond market accounted for 40 per cent of non-financial private sector's credit demand, the rest being covered by bank lending.

In recent years, long-term interest rates have declined in line with international developments (Diagram 4). Secondary-market bond yields came down from an average of 7.7 per cent in 1985 to 6.6 per cent in the first half of 1988. The downward movement, however, did not proceed smoothly. Preceded by steep yield increases in the German secondary market, bond prices fell in the third quarter of 1987. The (temporary) rise in long-term interest rates, however, came later and was less marked. Foreign investors increasingly turned to the Austrian bond market in response to the uncertainties created by the announcement of the introduction in 1989 of an interest withholding tax in Germany. Moreover, as in other countries, the bond market benefited from portfolio shifts in the wake of the stock-market crash, and, by the end of 1987, earlier price declines had been partially made up.

Diagram 4. **LONG-TERM BOND YIELDS**

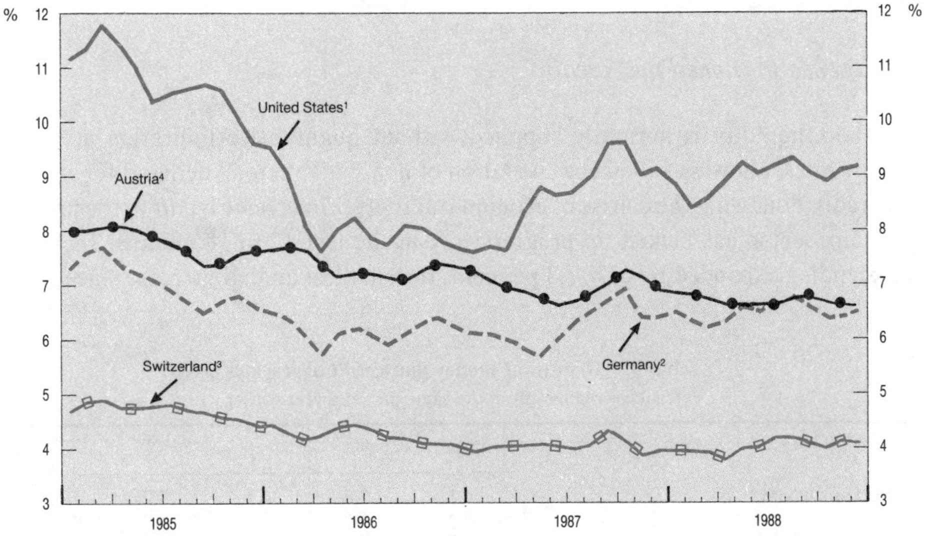

1. US government bonds (composite over 10 years).
2. 7-15 year public sector bonds.
3. Confederation bonds.
4. Public sector bonds.
Source: OECD, *Financial Statistics.*

The upward trend in bond prices continued in the first half of 1988, reflecting "scarcity" of Government debt supply, as increased federal debt financing, as noted above, was obtained from foreign sources. Bond prices fell somewhat over the summer, in response to higher domestic money market rates and the further rise in international long-term interest rates. However, since mid-August, bond yields have stabilised again, mirroring international developments. As a result, the yield differential *vis-à-vis* German rates, which amounted to ¾ per cent in January, disappeared in August 1988.

In the first ten months of 1988, total bond issues (excluding federal government obligations) amounted to Sch. 57 billion, 13 per cent more than in the same period in 1987. This marked buoyancy reflected a general trend towards investment in securities at the expense of monetary capital formation, as well as domestic banks' heavy demand for investment certificates. However, non-bank purchases of foreign currency-denominated securities have increased dramatically in 1988, prompted by the introduction of a 10 per cent withholding tax as from January 1989, more pronounced portfolio diversification on the part of non-financial investors and a "supply-gap" on the domestic market. In October 1988, prices on the Austrian stock market were 18½ per cent higher than at the beginning of the year, and the cumulative turnover of the first nine months of 1988 was 16 per cent higher than in the same period of 1987.

Trends in money and credit

Bank liquidity is normally supplied without quantitative limitation at given interest rates, allowing full accommodation of non-bank sectors' demand for money and credit. Following the course of economic activity, *direct bank credit* to the private non-bank sector has picked up progressively in the last 12 to 18 months. In 1987, bank lending expanded by only 7.3 per cent, the smallest annual increase since 1983

Table 3. **Growth of money and credit aggregates**

Percentage changes from the same period a year earlier

	1986	1987	1988		
			Q1	Q2	Q3
Central bank money	6.5	−2.5	6.4	5.7	6.5
Enlarged monetary base[1]	4.5	6.6	6.9	6.9	5.8
Money supply (M1)	4.6	9.4	9.7	8.4	8.1
Bank lending to the private sector	10.0	7.3	8.5	7.7	7.3

1. The enlarged monetary base includes notes and coins in circulation, banks' balances with the central bank and a minimum reserve adjustment.
Source: Österreichische Nationalbank, *Austria's Monetary Situation.*

(Table 3). Apart from sluggish economic activity, this also reflected changes in banking legislation, which called for a larger equity base and for banks to give profitability a higher priority and business volumes a lower one. Lending to industry fell (by ½ per cent), while public sector and personal borrowers' demands for funds remained buoyant (both categories increasing by 11 per cent). With the broadly-based strengthening of economic growth in 1988, demand for credit has increased. Credit to the household sector expanded strongly, while larger industrial firms with improving balance sheets had less recourse to banks for financing investment projects. However, including small-scale industry and crafts, there has been a noticeable increase in lending to the total business sector. The public sector, by contrast, has resorted significantly less to direct credit, reflecting a more intensive tapping of foreign markets, as well as the conjuncturally-induced reduction in the federal government's borrowing requirement.

In spite of subdued economic activity in 1987, and hence moderate need for transaction balances, monetary growth accelerated, reflecting an upward shift in the liquidity preference of portfolio holders. The *enlarged monetary base* expanded some 6.6 per cent, while the growth of the broader aggregates was more rapid, M2 topping at 13.7 per cent, with M3 and M1 at 9.6 and 9.4 per cent, respectively. These divergences reflected capital inflows from abroad and portfolio shifts within monetary capital formation, induced by rather low returns and uncertainty about future interest rate trends. In 1988, the expansion of the enlarged monetary base slowed after mid-year to less than 6 per cent on average over a year earlier, reflecting, among other things, a greater propensity of domestic non-banks to invest in financial assets which are not subject to minimum reserve requirements (in particular investment certificates). In contrast, the narrowly-defined money stock, M1, continued to grow strongly, with a higher transactions demand for money more than offsetting the restraining effects from higher interest rates. The broader aggregates, however, expanded more slowly, as acquisitions of time and savings deposits stagnated or even declined, as is normal in a phase of increasing economic activity.

Supply-side policies: progress and outstanding problems

Over the past two years, the Government has made progress in improving the supply side of the economy in several areas: restructuring of the *nationalised industries*; increasing private participation in and *sales of assets* of public enterprises; passing of the 1989 *income tax reform*; first steps in reducing indirect as well as direct *subsidies*; and further *deregulation* in financial markets including elimination in 1989 of virtually all reservations to the OECD code of capital movements.

Restructuring of nationalised industries (ÖIAG)

Nationalised industries within the ÖIAG-group form an important part of Austria's economy. In 1987, they accounted for 17 per cent of Austrian exports (21 per cent in 1980) and 3.5 per cent of dependent employment. The share of the nationalised sector is particularly high (more than 90 per cent of employees) in iron and steel and the oil industry, followed by mining, non-ferrous metals and foundries (employment shares of a third and more). In other important branches of industry, such as mechanical engineering, iron and metal products, and in the chemical and electrical industries, the employment share exceeds 10 per cent.

As noted in last year's Survey, it was not until the early 1980s that persistent losses in the nationalised sector led to a reduction of capacity. Employment was reduced much in line with that in private industry until 1985 (12 per cent and 10 per cent respectively). However, while the adjustment in the private sector had run its course by that time, as evidenced by a stabilisation of employment, further cut-backs took place in the nationalised sector. From 1985 to 1987, employment was curtailed by 20 000 employees or 20 per cent of the workforce. At the same time, the share of the ÖIAG group in industrial investment dropped from nearly 28 per cent in 1980 to under 23 per cent in 1987. Nevertheless, until 1986, the Federal Government made some Sch. 26 billion available to ÖIAG to support restructuring and to make up for unprofitable activities, including losses from oil speculation. The 1987 Financing Law provided additional transfers of Sch. 33 billion of which the major part was used as capital infusions to ÖIAG companies. This financial assistance was given, along with a restructuring plan which aimed at reaching a break-even situation by 1990 for the group as a whole and included a warning that no further funds would be made available thereafter.

The restructuring of ÖIAG has now been almost completed. This has involved a new investment strategy, a further drive towards internationalisation of activities and an overall reorganisation of the holding company. Priority in the holding's new investment programme has been shifted towards branches with better-than-average growth prospects. The internationalisation plan, which aims at securing jobs by gaining access to new markets abroad and to foreign technologies and products, is partly geared to the establishment of closer links with the European Community.

The ÖIAG companies have been regrouped according to their activities into seven functional holdings: mining, machinery and plant engineering, electronics,

24

steel, non-ferrous metals, oil, and chemicals. By end-1988, all these holdings were given a legal status. The seven holding companies, covering 350 companies, are headed by ÖIAG. Clearer lines of responsibility have been created in order to make operating units more responsive to market forces, by strengthening management control and reducing political interference. ÖIAG designs its overall strategy and controls the strategic and operative leadership of each daughter-holding, which in turn is responsible for the strategic and operative leadership of its producing companies. The managing staff and decision-making processes should become less politicized over time and nationalised companies are expected to be run according to standard business principles and practices. Balance-sheet losses in 1988 are estimated to have dwindled to less than Sch. 3 billion from Sch. 8 billion in 1987 and a peak of Sch. 12 billion in 1986. On a current transactions basis, 1988 is likely to close with a gross operating surplus of Sch. 1 billion, compared with a loss of more than Sch. 10 billion in 1987. About half of the improvement can be attributed to the favourable demand and price situation while the remainder reflects rationalisation and consolidation efforts.

Asset sales

As part of the overall economic strategy, but also in order to enlarge its financial room for manœuvre, the Government embarked upon a programme of selling shares of some nationalised companies. In the first instance, asset sales concerned companies whose main activity fell outside the broad production lines of the holding company. The proceeds of partial privatisation until 1988 amounted to some Sch. 5 billion including 15 per cent of the shares of the Austrian mineral oil company, ÖMV, about 18 per cent of the ÖIAG participation in Siemens Austria, and the sale of some peripheral companies (Table 4). Apart from these "peripheral" companies, asset sales have not meant a loss of majority control of public enterprises.

Important companies outside ÖIAG are controlled by state-owned banks such as the Creditanstalt and the Österreichische Länderbank. The Federal Government is currently reducing its share in these banks, though retaining the majority of the stock. Part of other large state-owned corporations, Austrian Airlines and the electricity companies, was offered for sale to the public in 1987 and/or 1988. Here too, the minimum stake of the federal government was kept at 51 per cent. Asset sales yielded only some Sch. 3 billion in 1988, Sch. 1½ billion less than budgeted for, but are intended to be continued in the next few years. In 1989, the National Bank will buy the Mint for Sch. 8 billion, while other partial privatisations, including the sale of shares of Creditanstalt, Länderbank and Verbundgesellschaft, are expected to provide additional revenue of Sch. 4 billion.

25

Table 4. **Asset sales, 1987-1989**

	Participation		Proceeds Sch. billion
	1986	1989	
	Per cent		
Federal government (1987-89)			
Austrian Electricity Company[1]	100	51	
Illwerke	70.2	51	} 9.9
Other smaller electricity companies	74.2	0	
Mint[2]	100	0	8.0
Creditanstalt-Bankverein[3]	60	51	0.2
Länderbank[3]	60	51	
Austrian Airlines[3]	99.2	51	0.7
Other	–	0	0.6
Total	–	–	19.3
ÖIAG (1987-88)			
Austrian Mineral Oil Company (ÖMV)	100	85	1.3
Siemens, Österreich	43.6	26	1.9
Other	–	–	1.9
Total	–	–	4.6

1. One-third of the central-state-owned shares are to be sold to the Länder.
2. Bought by the Austrian National Bank.
3. Net of capital infusions.
Source : Ministry of Finance.

The 1989 tax reform

In January 1989, a comprehensive *tax reform* has taken effect, involving a lowering of both direct personal and corporate tax rates, as well as a broadening of the tax base. The main reasons for the reform were the growing difficulties of achieving redistribution aims, the erosion of the tax base and distortions to incentives to work, save and invest emanating from the tax structure. Important reforms have also taken place in the United States, Japan, the United Kingdom and Germany, where general features included a lowering of top marginal income tax rates, a reduced number of tax brackets, and the reduction or elimination of a number of tax reliefs. In Austria, as can be seen from Table 5, the top marginal personal income tax rate is now in the medium range, whereas the bottom rate is the lowest (the same as in Japan and Italy). The corporation tax rate is the lowest among the countries considered.

The new tax system, which is discussed in more detail in Part III, is on balance expected to have a number of beneficial *supply-side effects*. The lowering of marginal income tax rates could enhance *labour supply*, while less favourable rules with respect

Table 5. **Tax reform : an international comparison**

| | Tax cuts (central government) | | | | Widening the tax base through tax expenditure cuts | Partial compensation of revenue losses through increased consumption taxes | Revenue neutral |
| | Households income taxes | | Corporation taxes[1] | | | | |
	Before reform	After	Before reform	After			
Austria	21 % to 62 %	10 % to 50 % (1989)	30 % to 55 %	30 % (1989)	sizeable	yes	no
Germany	22 % to 56 %	19 % to 53 % (1990)	56 %	50 % (1990)	sizeable	yes (1989)	no
United States	11 % to 50 %	2 rates : 15 % and 28 % ; and increase in tax allowances for low-income brackets (1986)	46 %	34 % (1986)	sizeable	no	essentially
Japan	10.5 % to 60 % (1987)	10 % to 50 % (1989)	42 % (1988)	37.5 % (1990+)	limited	Introduction of generalised VAT at a rate of 3 %	no
United Kingdom	29 % to 60 %	2 rates : 20 % and 40 % (1988)	35 %	35 %	limited	yes	no
Canada	6 % to 34 %	3 rates : 17 %, 26 % and 29 % and tax credit to replace tax allowances (1988)	36 %	28 % (1988)	yes	yes	yes
Netherlands	16 % to 72 %	3 rates : 35 %, 52 % and 60 % including social security contributions	42 %	35 %	essentially	no	essentially

Note : The years in brackets indicate the date of implementation of the tax reform.
1. Undistributed profits.
Source : OECD.

to overtime might pull in the opposite direction. While incentives to work might be increased by the reduced progressivity of the tax system, the positive effects on private household *savings* from the rise in disposable incomes could be partly offset by the simultaneous reduction in savings-promotion and a new capital income tax on household revenues from financial investment. *Capital formation* will mainly be stimulated through stronger after-tax profitability outweighing the negative effect of rising user-cost of capital. According to a study by WIFO (WIFO, 1988), the new tax system will mainly favour investments with a shorter lifetime, which may accelerate the renewal and enhance the technological quality of the capital stock. The willingness to incur risk may also be increased by lower company taxation and taxation of income from low-risk monetary assets, at the same time favouring the enlargement of firms' capital base.

Deregulation and subsidies

In contrast to achievements in the fields of the nationalised industries and tax reform, comparatively little progress has so far been made in the areas of deregulation and direct subsidies. A new *cartel law* was adopted, aimed at creating greater transparency with regard to competitive conditions and reducing possibilities for establishing restrictive business practices. It has also been decided to dismantle progressively in 1989 most of the existing reservations to the OECD code on capital flows, which should help to internationalise Austrian industry and strengthen financial integration, and hence competition in the financial sector. However, measures to open up competition of small industry, crafts and some service sectors such as transportation and banking have been modest so far. This has recently been underscored by a study (Ministry of Finance, 1988) which found that entry requirements and professional regulations severely affect competition in 220 professions and trades. Moreover, sectors representing 40 per cent of GDP are currently subject to detailed regulation in the Trade Regulations Law (Gewerbeordnung) and in similar legislation (goods transportation, banks, insurance). According to the study, the existing web of regulations has proven inefficient in achieving initial aims in the area of consumer protection, protection of standards in liberal professions, and prevention of "unfair" competition. This has led to higher prices than would otherwise have been the case, a slowdown of structural adjustment, and more generally, a reduction of competitive forces. The main recommendation is that a genuine overhaul of the regulatory framework would significantly contribute to increasing the transparency of markets, the efficiency of the producing sectors and the dynamism of the economy at large.

28

Subsidies to the business sector are pervasive and comprise a wide range of schemes covering the entire spectrum of economic sectors. On a national accounts basis, subsidies amounted to Sch. 46.7 billion in 1987 or about 3 per cent of GDP, which is not particularly high by international comparison. Including capital transfers would, however, be significantly higher. Indirect subsidies *via* tax expenditures have also been important. The tax reform should curtail these forms of subsidisation appreciably.

Table 6. **Subsidies**

Schilling billion

	1985		1986		1987	
	Total Government	Federal Government	Total Government	Federal Government	Total Government	Federal Government
Direct subsidies						
Agriculture	. .	8.1	. .	8.9	. .	9.8
Enterprises[1]	. .	7.6	. .	6.7	. .	6.1
Total	. .	15.7	.	15.6	. .	15.9
Indirect subsidies						
Agriculture	4.7	2.3	4.8	2.3	4.8	2.4
Enterprises[1]	21.8	15.2	23.5	16.3	25.0	17.1
Total	26.5	17.5	28.3	18.6	29.8	19.5

1. Including liberal trade.
Source : Ministry of Finance, *Förderungsbericht 1987*.

Industry (including the nationalised sector) and agriculture have been the main beneficiaries, but housing too is heavily supported. Federal direct subsidies, as accounted for in the Budget Report, have in recent years grown in line with GDP (Table 6). However, various programmes favouring specific kinds of investment through grants, interest subsidies, favourable loan conditions or earmarked revenues have been scaled back. In the 1989 Budget further moderate steps to reduce subsidisation have been taken. Moreover, the freeze on transfers to agriculture imposed in 1988 has been maintained, implying a cut in real terms.

II. Economic developments in 1988 and the outlook to 1990

1988: timely dynamism

Since the middle of 1987, economic growth has regained considerable strength. Following two years of near-stagnation, industrial output picked up towards the end of 1987. The resilience of the world economy to the October 1987 stock market crash, together with the renewed buoyancy of world trade, has given a strong boost to business and consumer confidence. Helped by temporary factors, the upswing gathered further momentum in 1988, with real GDP expanding by 4 per cent, the highest rate since the beginning of this decade and slightly higher than the average for the smaller European OECD Member countries (Diagram 5).

Positive stimuli from abroad

Much of the strength of the economy, which was largely unexpected a year ago, originated from international developments. Apart from higher economic activity in trading partner countries which boosted demand for Austrian products, there has been a shift of foreign demand towards raw materials and intermediate goods, which constitute a large part of the product-mix of the Austrian export sector. The stabilisation of the effective schilling exchange rate, entailed by a weakening of the Deutschemark against the dollar since early 1988, has strengthened international cost-competitiveness, while at the same time permitting some widening of profit margins.

Following a modest 1½ per cent increase in 1987, *exports of goods and services* in volume increased by 7½ per cent in 1988, or nearly 6½ percentage points more than projected in last year's Survey. Exports of steel, wood and metal products, were most buoyant, while, in line with past cyclical experience, the pick-up in investment goods

Diagram 5.   **REAL GDP IN AUSTRIA AND ABROAD**

Growth rates

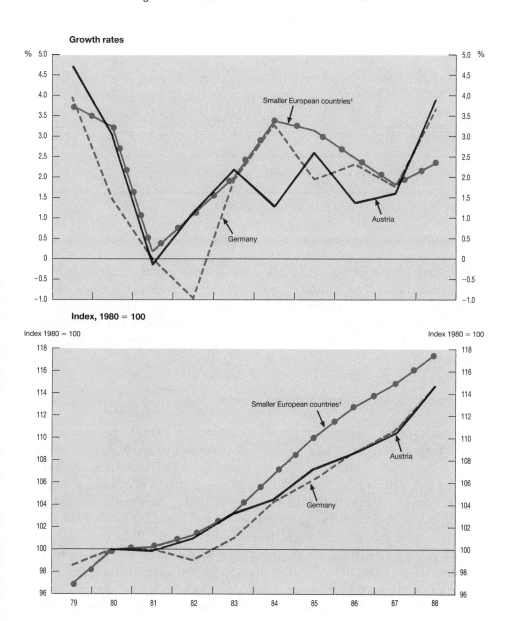

1.   Weighted average of Belgium, Denmark, Finland, Norway, Sweden and Switzerland.
Sources: OECD, *National Accounts* and OECD estimates.

31

Table 7. **Exports and competitiveness in manufacturing**

Percentage changes

	1985	1986	1987	1988
Volumes				
Exports	9.8	1.1	2.0	8.5
Export markets	4.4	5.1	6.7	7.8
Relative export performance[1]	5.2	-3.8	-4.4	0.7
Prices				
Export prices (local currency)	3.3	-2.6	-2.4	0.8
Unit labour costs	1.7	3.7	1.7	-0.1
Profit margins[2]	1.6	-6.1	-4.0	0.9

1. Export growth divided by export market growth.
2. Export price growth divided by unit labour cost growth.
Source: OECD, *Economic Outlook 44*, December 1988.

occurred only later in the year. All in all, manufacturing exports increased by 8½ per cent, slightly faster than Austrian markets (Table 7). Although the new customs trade reporting system has blurred trade statistics since the beginning of 1988, it seems that market share gains have been particularly marked in Germany, France, Spain and the United Kingdom. In volume terms, exports of services grew by some 4 per cent.

Broadly-based domestic demand growth

Total domestic demand increased by 4½ per cent in 1988, 1¾ percentage point faster than in 1987. Except for government purchases of goods and services, all demand components shared the reacceleration (Table 8). The surge in household spending took place against the backdrop of slowing growth of nominal disposable income, from 5½ per cent in 1987 to 4 per cent in 1988. *Compensation of employees* grew by only 3¼ per cent. Tax payments, which had remained flat in 1987 as tax allowances were increased, resumed more normal growth. With consumer price inflation picking up slightly, the advance of *real disposable income* was more than halved. Even so, financed by dissaving and greater willingness to incur debt, there has been a spending spree for consumer durables, which pushed the volume of private consumption up by 3½ per cent between 1987 and 1988. As a result, following a rise of 4½ percentage points to 12¾ per cent in the two years to 1987, the household saving ratio declined to 11¼ per cent, and bank lending to private households expanded by some 15 per cent.

Table 8. **Demand and output**

Volumes, 1976 prices, percentage changes

	1985	1986	1987	1988
Private consumption	2.2	1.6	2.4	3.5
Government consumption	2.3	1.6	0.7	0.5
Gross fixed investment	4.9	3.6	1.8	5.3
Construction	0.7	3.5	3.1	4.5
Machinery and equipment	9.9	3.8	1.0	6.0
Final domestic demand	2.8	2.1	2.0	3.4
Stockbuilding[1,2]	−0.2	0.8	0.8	1.2
Total domestic demand	2.6	2.9	2.7	4.6
Exports of goods and services	6.9	−3.2	1.6	7.5
Imports of goods and services	6.9	0.2	4.4	8.8
Foreign balance[1]	0.1	−1.5	−1.2	−0.6
GDP	2.6	1.4	1.5	4.0
Memorandum items :				
Consumption deflator	3.5	2.0	0.9	1.9
GDP deflator	2.9	4.1	2.6	1.6
Industrial production	4.5	1.1	0.6	4.5
Productivity	2.6	0	1.0	3.0

1. Changes in stockbuilding and the foreign balance are expressed as a per cent of GDP in the previous period.
2. Including the statistical discrepancy.
Sources : Österreichisches Statistisches Zentralamt, *Österreichs Volkseinkommen,* and OECD estimates for 1988.

The reduction of the *household saving ratio* in 1988 seems to mark a return to a more normal savings behaviour, prompted by better-than-expected labour market developments and continuing low inflation. To some extent, however, it may also reflect advanced purchases prior to the introduction of the 1989 tax reform. Over the 15 years to 1985, household savings as a percentage of disposable income declined by 4 points to just over 8 per cent, much in line with international developments (Diagram 6). This weakening propensity to save may be attributable to improved social protection, rising real pension benefits and less precautionary saving in the face of persistently low unemployment. In addition, the advent of the post-World War II baby-boom generation on the labour market has entailed a lowering of the average age of the labour force. In a life-cycle consumption framework, this would also explain the decline in the average household saving ratio. The discontinuation of this trend in 1986 and 1987, when the saving ratio jumped back to its level of the early 1970s, may be related to the fact that a large part of the real income gains in these two years resulted from imported disinflation and lower "home-made" inflation. Indeed, as experienced in other countries too, consumption seems more responsive to real

33

Diagram 6. **THE SAVING RATIO IN SELECTED OECD COUNTRIES**
(Per cent of disposable income)

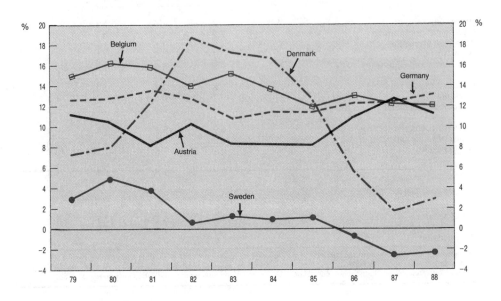

Sources: OECD, *National Accounts* and OECD estimates.

income gains generated by nominal income growth than to increases due to reduced inflation. Moreover, consumer demand was damped by the cyclical weakness of overall economic activity and probably also by increased uncertainty about future income and employment prospects. To a large extent, the renewed decline in the saving ratio in 1988 reflects the unwinding of these special factors.

Stronger *capital formation* also played an important role in the rebound of domestic demand. Investment activity was favoured by clement weather conditions in the early part of 1988, and buoyed up by advancement effects in response to the introduction of the new tax system in 1989, which abolishes accelerated depreciation facilities and makes housing promotion schemes less favourable (see Part III). More fundamental influences were better profit developments and improved domestic demand and export prospects. Construction activity was quite buoyant, though slightly less than investment in machinery and equipment, reflecting not only good

34

weather conditions but also pent-up housing demand following protracted sluggishness during most of the 1980s. Stockbuilding has lent strong support to total demand, but contrary to 1987, when there was an important involuntary build-up of inventories, its continued strength in 1988 seems to be due primarily to better medium-term sales prospects.

Imports and output growth

Reflecting the pick-up in total domestic demand, the volume growth of *imports* of goods and services accelerated sharply in 1988. Imports of raw materials were strongest and there was a turnaround in non-tourism services. The drag of the real foreign balance on output growth was smaller in 1988 than in 1987, permitting *real GDP* to increase no less than 4 per cent, more than twice the rate achieved in the previous year. Manufacturing industries benefited most from the better economic climate, with production increasing by some 4½ per cent. Intermediate goods industries led the upswing, followed later by investment goods.

Moderately improving labour market

Contrary to expectations a year ago, the labour market showed some improvement in 1988 (Table 9). Thanks to a turnaround of the decline in self-employment and faster growth of dependent employment, total *employment*

Table 9. **Labour market developments**
Percentage changes

	1981	1982	1983	1984	1985	1986	1987	1988
Population of working age	1.0	0.9	0.4	0.7	0.5	0.4	0.4	0.3
Total labour force	0.6	−0.1	−0.1	0.2	1.1	1.1	0.6	0.4
Total employment	−0.2	−1.4	−0.9	0	0.2	0.3	−0.1	0.6
Dependent employment	0.4	−1.2	−1.1	0.4	0.6	0.7	0.2	0.8
Industry	−2.1	−4.1	−4.1	−0.8	0.2	−0.6	−2.7	−2.2
Foreign workers	−1.7	−9.2	−6.8	−4.6	1.1	4.1	1.0	2.7
Thousands								
Registered unemployed	69	105	127	130	139	152	165	160
Unfilled vacancies	25	17	15	17	22	25	27	31
Unemployment rate[1]	2.4	3.7	4.5	4.5	4.8	5.2	5.6	5.4

1. Registered unemployed as a per cent of dependent labour force.
Sources: Ministry of Social Affairs, *Arbeitsmarktvorschau 1989*, Österreichisches Institut für Wirtschaftsforschung and OECD estimates.

growth, though modest by international comparison, was the highest since 1979. Labour productivity accelerated from an average rate of ½ per cent in 1986-87 to 3 per cent, despite a shift of employment from capital-intensive industries to services. The contraction of employment in industry continued, but average hours worked seem to have increased somewhat. With stronger demand for less-qualified and part-time labour in the service sector, dependent employment of women increased faster than that of men.

In both 1987 and 1988, the labour force increased at about the same rate as the population of working age, with falling male participation rates broadly offset by increasing female participation. New job creation exceeded the increase in the labour force in 1988 for the first time since the early 1980s, resulting in some decline in unemployment. Female unemployment rates remained marginally higher than male rates. The share of youth unemployment (aged 15 to 24 years) in total unemployment was reduced by 5½ percentage points between 1986 and 1988, reversing the previous upward trend.

Maintenance of a high degree of price stability

The disinflation process came to a halt in 1988 (Table 10). Under the impact of falling world energy and commodity prices, the rise in the private consumption deflator reached its nadir of less than 1 per cent in 1987, the lowest rate in nineteen years. With import prices picking up and a number of indirect taxes increased, consumer-price inflation reaccelerated to a rate of 2 per cent during 1988, despite further moderation of labour-cost pressures. Indeed, nominal wage increases came down from 5.5 per cent in 1986 to 2.7 per cent in 1988, reflecting lagged responses to lower inflation, deteriorating labour market conditions, and difficulties in nationalised industries.

Table 10. **Prices and costs**

Percentage changes

	1985	1986	1987	1988
Wage rate, total economy	5.2	5.5	3.8	2.7
Hourly earnings in manufacturing	5.7	4.5	5.0	3.3
Unit labour costs, total economy	3.3	4.6	2.4	−0.7
Import prices	3.2	−7.0	−3.4	1.3
Terms of trade	0.1	5.7	2.5	0.6
Private consumption deflator	3.5	2.0	0.9	2.0
GDP deflator	2.9	4.1	2.6	1.6

Sources: Österreichisches Statistisches Zentralamt, and OECD estimates.

Domestically-generated inflation remained limited in 1988 as slowing growth of nominal wages went hand-in-hand with stronger productivity growth. However, profit margins seem to have widened, entailing a faster rise in the GDP deflator than in unit labour costs in 1988. In this context it may be noted that since 1981, the average annual rise in manufacturing unit labour costs has been ½ per cent lower than in Germany, reflecting better productivity performance rather than slower nominal wage growth. Moreover, the evolution of profits has been better in Austria.

Slightly worsening balance of payments

After approximate balance in 1986, the *current external account* has since swung back into a small deficit (Table 11). With both export and, above all, import prices falling significantly, the traditional *trade deficit* contracted in 1987. It shrank a little further in 1988 when terms-of-trade gains dropped sharply. The decline of the surplus on *services and transfers* came to a halt in 1988, largely thanks to higher receipts on tourism. The steady fall of overnight stays of foreigners observed since 1981 stopped in 1987, giving way to a moderate increase in 1988. At the same time, the drift towards higher-quality accommodation and growing city tourism has kept average expenditure per visitor rising. Despite a surge in Austrian tourist spending abroad, the

Table 11. **The current external balance**
Schilling billion

	1986	1987	1988
Exports	332	343	375
Imports	399	396	429
Trade balance	−67	−53	−52
Investment income, net	−10	−11	−10
Non-factor services, net	76	63	61
Transfers, net	1	−1	−1
Current balance	1	−3	−2
Memorandum items :			
Change in the trade balance	14	16	1
of which :			
Due to terms-of-trade changes	26	29	9
Due to volume changes	−12	−13	−8
Balance on tourism[1]	45	45	43

1. National definitions, OECD estimate for 1988.
Sources : Österreichische Nationalbank, and OECD, *Economic Outlook 44,* December 1988.

surplus in the balance on tourism is estimated to have remained virtually stable in 1988 after a significant fall in 1987. The deficit on investment income also appears to have hardly changed despite rising interest payments on public foreign debt. In dollar terms, the current deficit was a little over US $¼ billion in both 1987 and 1988 (less than ¼ per cent of GDP).

The outlook for 1989 and 1990

Technical assumptions

The main features of the international background as discussed in greater detail in the recent OECD, *Economic Outlook 44*, are summarised in Table 12. The growth of world import volumes is projected to decelerate only moderately and Austrian market growth – at around 7 per cent 1989 and 1990 – should remain much in line with developments of the two preceding years. The price of oil is assumed to remain unchanged in real terms and the effective exchange rate to stay at the level of 4th November 1988 (Sch. 12.53 per U.S. dollar). The rise in import prices is projected to remain moderate, though edging up to 1 per cent in 1989 and 2 per cent in 1990.

The OECD projections are based on present and announced policies (Table 13). As noted above, *fiscal policy* is now set on a medium-term consolidation path, aiming at reducing the federal deficit to 2½ per cent of GDP by 1992. The budget proposal for 1989 suggests, however, that, contrary to developments in 1988, fiscal policy will

Table 12. **Technical assumptions, 1989 and 1990**

Percentage changes from previous period

	1988	1989	1990
Volumes			
World merchandise trade	8.9	7½	7
Manufacturing export markets	7.8	7	7 ¼
Prices			
Effective exchange rate			
Indices, 1982=100	112.8	113	113¼
Per cent change	0.2	¼	¼
Import prices	0	1	2

Source : OECD, *Economic Outlook 44*, December 1988.

38

Table 13. **Policy assumptions, 1989 and 1990**

Per cent of GDP

	1988	1989	1990
General government budget balance (Sch. billion)	–2.7	–3	–2½
Change in structural budget balance (per cent of GDP)[1]	0.2	–3¾	¼

1. Indicates whether the structural budget balance strengthens (+) or weakens (−).
Source: OECD, estimates and projections.

add to demand growth in 1989. In terms of the change in the cyclically-adjusted general government balance, the expansionary move is estimated at about ¾ per cent of GDP. For 1990, according to official statements, budget consolidation policies are assumed to be pursued with greater determination, with the main emphasis being on expenditure restraint. Despite a slower expansion of economic activity, revenue growth may be sufficiently boosted by lagged effects of the 1989 tax reform to bring the general government deficit down to 2½ per cent of GDP. *Monetary policy* is assumed to continue to operate within the hard-currency option, implying that Austrian interest rates should move in sympathy with German interest rates.

Wage settlements. Given the only modest improvement in labour market conditions in 1988 and taking account of reported local shortages of certain categories of qualified labour, the growth of effective wages for the economy as a whole may pick up from 2¾ per cent in 1988 to 3½ per cent in both 1989 and 1990. This would be the net result from very low increases in public sector wages (in line with government policy) and faster increases in the private sector, where the healthy profits recorded in 1988 may give rise to higher wage claims and somewhat more aggressive trade-union attitudes.

The outlook to 1990: continued, but slower economic growth

Following strong growth in 1988, overall output is expected to expand at an average rate of 2½ per cent in 1989 and 1990. Positive stimuli to economic activity are expected to come both from abroad and from domestic demand (Table 14). The projected growth of Austrian export markets should ensure continued buoyancy of *exports of goods and services.* On wage developments as outlined above, international competitiveness, measured by relative unit labour costs in common currency, should remain unchanged over the projection period while relative export prices could even

39

Table 14. **Projections for 1989 and 1990**

Volumes, 1976 prices, percentage changes

	1988	1989	1990
Private consumption	3.5	3½	2½
Government consumption	0.5	½	½
Gross fixed investment	5.2	3½	3
Construction	4.5	2	2¼
Machinery and equipment	6.0	5	3½
Final domestic demand	3.4	3	2¼
Stockbuilding[1,2]	1.3	¼	0
Total domestic demand	4.5	3	2¼
Exports of goods and services	7.5	5½	5
Imports of goods and services	8.8	6	5
Foreign balance[1]	−0.7	−¼	0
GDP	4.0	2¾	2¼
Memorandum items :			
Private consumption deflator	2.0	2¾	2½
GDP deflator	1.6	2½	2¼
Unemployment rate[3]	3.7	3¾	3¾
Current balance			
Schilling billion	−2.0	−1¼	½
U.S. dollars billion	−0.2	0	0

1. Changes as a per cent of GDP in the previous period.
2. Including the statistical discrepancy.
3. As a per cent of total labour force.
Source : OECD projections.

decline. Capacity constraints might emerge in some industries and in tourism; probably more importantly, however, export growth is likely to be damped by a reduction in the share of world demand accounted for by raw materials and intermediate goods. As a result, small market-share losses might occur in both 1989 and 1990.

While remaining broadly based, *domestic demand* growth is likely to slow over the projection period. In 1989, boosted by the introduction of the tax reform, households' disposable incomes may increase in real terms at some 3 per cent, but income gains in 1990 could well be halved. However, a further unwinding of the high saving ratio may prevent growth of consumer demand from falling below 2½ per cent. Capital accumulation is projected to slow down reflecting temporary distortions of investment expenditure flows due to the introduction of the tax reform and a cyclical downturn in residential construction. The underlying expansion in business investment may moderate as desired capital/output ratios are approached. No further significant contribution from stockbuilding to domestic demand growth is likely. Government demand for goods and services can be expected to be severely constrained by closer adherence to medium-term targets.

In line with slower domestic demand growth, the rise in *import volumes* should moderate. This may leave the real foreign balance roughly unchanged in both 1989 and 1990, with *real GDP* growth staying at around 2 to 2½ per cent in these years. Employment growth should match the modest increase in the labour force, leaving the unemployment rate unchanged. With import price increases likely to remain modest and restrained wage settlements, *inflation* is projected to remain virtually stable at some 2½ per cent.

With terms-of-trade gains projected to dwindle in 1989 and disappear in 1990, the *trade deficit* could increase somewhat from $4¼ billion in 1988 to $5 billion in 1990. Some further improvement is expected for the services account, so that the current external account could return to approximate balance in 1990.

Risks and uncertainties

These projections are as usual surrounded by a number of risks and uncertainties. This applies both to international developments as well as to domestic prospects. Concerning the likely trends of the international economy, *Economic Outlook 44* stresses the risk that the current-account adjustment process among the largest OECD economies may come to a halt. This could at some point invalidate the technical assumption of unchanged effective exchange rates, and heighten the probability of exchange-rate-induced policy reactions across the OECD area which would be detrimental to growth of international trade. There are also inflation risks in a number of countries, which, if they become more pronounced, may alter policy settings and hence the outlook for world demand and activity growth. Turning to the domestic scene, the main uncertainty attaches to the likely development of private consumption and investment. If uncertainties increased about the maintenance of the real value of pensions in the future, the predicted lowering of the saving ratio might fail to materialise. A downward risk is also attached to the investment projections. At present the outlook is for fairly steady growth of capital formation through 1989 and 1990, but should exports turn out to be less buoyant than expected, investment demand would also probably be weaker.

III.   Public sector issues: tax reform and social security financing

Last year's Survey called for restraint in spending areas which place a particularly heavy burden on federal finances: the wage bill, pension payments and all forms of direct or indirect subsidisation of the economy. It was suggested that measures to increase the elasticity of tax revenues to rising incomes would facilitate the task of medium-term budget consolidation. This chapter first reviews some of the principal reasons for public-sector growth, and then examines the main features of the 1989 tax reform and the financing problems facing the social insurance system.

Growth and structure of government expenditure

Since the end of the post-war reconstruction period, the public sector has steadily increased in Austria as generally elsewhere. In relation to GDP, it is among the larger ones in the OECD area, surpassed by e.g. Belgium, Denmark, the Netherlands and Sweden. On a national-accounts basis, the share of total public spending in GDP rose from almost 36 per cent in 1960 to more than 52 per cent in 1987. In the 1950s, important infrastructure investment programmes were carried out. Since then, the expansion of the social security system has been the major source of growth. Moreover, counter-cyclical surges in public spending programmes, implemented to sustain high employment levels, have proven difficult to scale back in subsequent business upswings.

After the second oil crisis, most Member governments tried to restrain public sector growth, with more or less success. In most countries, public investment has been curtailed, the rapid expansion of the government wage bill arrested, and transfer payments have been brought more closely into line with overall wage growth. The

Diagram 7. **TOTAL PUBLIC EXPENDITURE NET OF INTEREST PAYMENTS**

(Per cent of GDP)

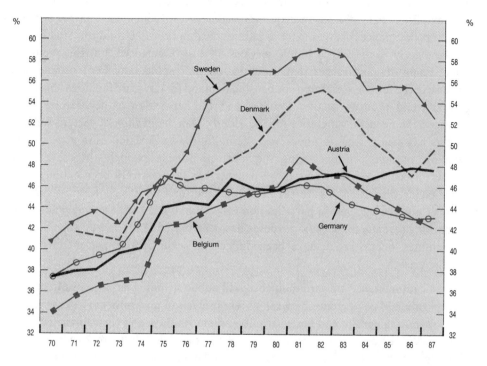

Source: OECD, *National Accounts.*

move towards budget consolidation came later in Austria and has been less pronounced than in a number of other countries where budgetary difficulties were viewed as being more dramatic. Indeed, even excluding net interest payments, Austria has experienced a virtually uninterrupted increase in public sector spending since the beginning of the 1970s, while, as shown in Diagram 7, a clear downturn had already started in the early 1980s in many other countries.

Demographic developments represent one of the principal reasons for the persistent growth in public outlays. In the 1960s and 1970s, the post-war baby-boom generation passed through the education system and entered the labour market. From the late 1960s, the number and share of young children began to drop while the number of older people and their share in the population began to increase. An additional important feature is the *downward rigidity* in public spending areas where demographic developments would have allowed a reduction in expenditure. Education is the most prominent case. The increase in standards, measured by the decrease in the pupil-teacher ratio, has been quite considerable, without always having been an explicit policy choice. In other fields of public consumption, like child care and homes for the elderly, *standards* of public services have also increased, but this seems to reflect rising demand rather than rigidities on the supply side. For example, the increase in the female workforce has boosted demand for day-care facilities. Also, the general trend towards smaller families and the separation of generations have increased the need for amenities for the elderly. The *indexation* of certain welfare benefits has also played an important role in "hardening" rigidities in government spending, old-age pensions being the most prominent example. Moreover, the number of people eligible for welfare benefits has progressively been extended by either policy discretion, e.g. to the self-employed, or by socio-economic-structure changes, e.g. the increase in participation rates. Finally, the widespread practice of earmarking revenue for specific purposes has contributed to ratchet-up spending, as programmes, once started, have been difficult to scale back in periods of slower revenue growth.

An "autonomous" upward momentum in public spending has also resulted from the separation of competence between different levels of government (federal versus local) regarding certain categories of public sector outlays and their financing. The best known example is the case of school-teachers (Landeslehrer), where local governments are responsible for recruitment and determine employment conditions, while the federal government has been legally obliged since 1973 to carry the burden of remuneration. Over the past few years, compensation of school teachers has accounted for 18 per cent of the total federal government wage bill. Similarly, loans for residential construction at preferential rates are extended by the Länder to households, while financing is at the charge of the federal budget. In 1987-88, such loans amounted to about Sch. 16 billion on average. To make the system more transparent, the financing of these loans by revenue sharing was replaced in 1988 by direct grants from the federal government.

Recent efforts to moderate the rise in public spending have taken place against the backdrop of rising interest rate payments on public debt. This has altered the *composition of public expenditure* (Diagram 8). Indeed, interest payments have grown steadily, chiefly at the expense of public investment, accounting for 10 per cent of total federal outlays in 1987. Even so, as a ratio to GDP, they are still low by international standards. Government consumption rose faster than GDP in the 1960s

44

Diagram 8. **STRUCTURE OF PUBLIC EXPENDITURE**

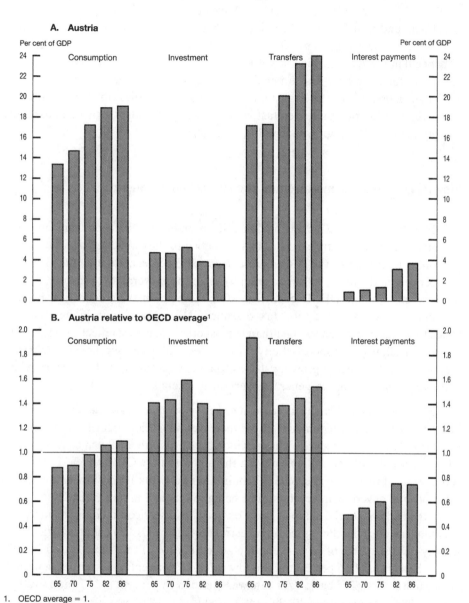

A. Austria

Per cent of GDP

Consumption   Investment   Transfers   Interest payments

B. Austria relative to OECD average[1]

Consumption   Investment   Transfers   Interest payments

65 70 75 82 86   65 70 75 82 86   65 70 75 82 86   65 70 75 82 86

1. OECD average = 1.
A value above/equal/lower than implies a share above/equal/lower than the OECD average; average calculated with United States, Canada, Japan, Austria, Belgium, Denmark, Finland, France, Germany, Italy, Norway, Spain, Sweden, United Kingdom.
Source: OECD, *National Accounts.*

and 1970s, while moving in parallel to nominal income growth in the 1980s. Seen in relation to developments in other OECD countries, public consumption (as a share of GDP) caught up with the average OECD level only in the early 1980s, while public investment and transfers have been higher than on average elsewhere. Government employment grew from about 10 per cent of total employment in 1960 to just over 20 per cent in 1987, roughly in line with the OECD average. Transfer payments to the private sector have been less amenable to efforts at restraint, as reflected in the persistent increase in the transfers/GDP ratio. Subsidies to agriculture and nationalised industries have risen fast, and transfer payments to private households, notably pensions, have grown steadily in real terms.

Financing public expenditure and the rise in indebtedness

In order to meet the increasing demands for public services and transfers, more and more financial resources had to be channelled to the public sector. The general government revenue-to-GDP ratio rose from 36½ per cent in the mid-1960s to 47½ per cent in the mid-1980s (Diagram 9). In terms of overall tax pressure, Austria ranks seventh among OECD countries, after the Scandinavian countries, Benelux and France. However, the total tax revenue/GDP ratio, though higher than the OECD average, increased less fast than in most other countries, reflecting a relatively low and declining revenue elasticity with respect to GDP (see below). A partial compensation has been a growing share of non-tax revenues, such as property and entrepreneurial income, in general government receipts.

Since the mid-1970s, the increase in *general government revenue* relative to GDP has primarily been accounted for by increases in social security contributions (Diagram 10). Social security charges increased from about 9 per cent to almost 14 per cent of GDP and are now among the highest in the OECD area. Income tax revenues rose broadly parallel to GDP, maintaining a virtually constant share (26 per cent) of total government receipts, thus being lower than in most OECD countries. Since the mid-1960s, the share of taxes on goods and services in GDP has increased only moderately, nonetheless leaving Austria among the OECD countries which rely heavily on this source of revenue. Value-added tax (VAT) was introduced in 1973 with a basic rate of 16 per cent and a low rate of 8 per cent for essential household needs such as food. The basic VAT rate was raised to 18 per cent in 1976 and to 20 per cent in 1984. The top rate of 30 per cent, introduced in 1978, was lifted to 32 per cent in 1984. In 1986, VAT receipts represented 65 per cent of taxes on goods and services.

46

Diagram 9. **PUBLIC SECTOR REVENUE TRENDS**
(Per cent of GDP)

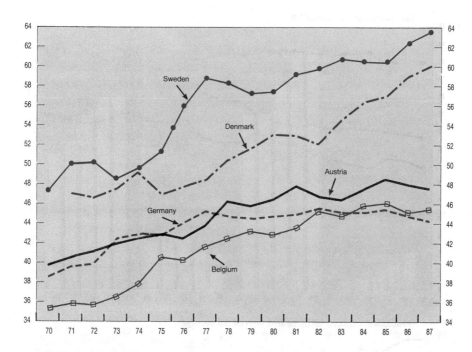

Source: OECD, *National Accounts.*

The different levels of government and individual social security funds each raise taxes and/or collect contributions. Part of the taxes raised by the federal government is redistributed to local authorities through the system of revenue-sharing. Each level of government and other legal bodies (funds and chambers) receive a fixed percentage of a given tax. Reflecting historical evolutions there is no overall rationale to the present tax-sharing system. Proceeds from the wealth tax and the corporate tax, for example, have accrued entirely to the central government, while other property and income-related taxes are shared between the three levels of government. Horizontal allocation among Länder as well as among municipalities is broadly effected according to the size of the population. In 1988, the federal government collected 67 per cent of all taxes (including tax-like revenue), local authorities,

Diagram 10. **STRUCTURE OF TAXATION**

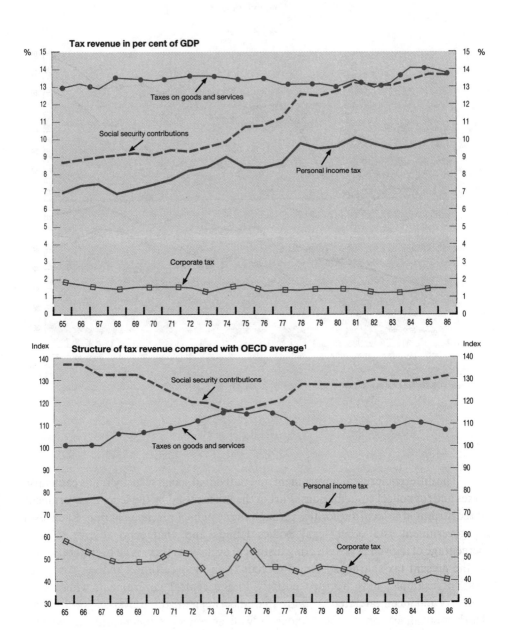

Tax revenue in per cent of GDP

Taxes on goods and services

Social security contributions

Personal income tax

Corporate tax

Structure of tax revenue compared with OECD average¹

Social security contributions

Taxes on goods and services

Personal income tax

Corporate tax

1. OECD average = 100.
Source: OECD, *Revenue Statistics of OECD Countries,* Paris, 1988.

48

Table 15. **Taxes by levels of government, 1988**

Schilling billion

	Federal government	Local authorities	Social security funds
Taxes collected[1]	440.6	30.6	179.7
of which :			
Revenue-sharing	–106.7	108.7[2]	–2.0
Net tax revenue	333.9	139.3	177.7

1. Including tax-like revenues.
2. Excluding transfers for promotion of residential construction.
Source : Ministry of Finance.

i.e. Länder, municipalities, as well as chambers and funds, raised 5 per cent of tax revenues and social security funds the rest (Table 15). Overall, a fourth of the taxes collected by the central government were redistributed to other levels of government.

Weakening direct tax responsiveness and tax distortions

One principal reason for the slow growth of government revenue has been the widening gap between statutory marginal and effective tax rates on total income. For an average income-earner, the spread, amounting to some 17 percentage points in the 1970s and early 1980s, rose to as much as 23 percentage points in 1987, largely as a result of increasingly generous tax credits and allowances, and tax exemptions. Indeed, excessive progressivity had created demands for tax concessions, whose marginal value rises with marginal tax rates. When granted, the tax base was eroded and a vicious circle was established. Moreover, the average effective rate of taxation has been reduced by preferential fiscal treatment of certain components of revenues, in particular by the low tax rates applicable to the 13th, 14th and, until 1988, also 15th month salary – 0 to 6 per cent according to family status for the 13th and 14th month salary – and the favourable tax treatment of severance pay, retirement bonuses and overtime pay. The erosion of the tax base has drastically reduced the responsiveness of the tax system to income growth in spite of a top marginal tax rate of 62 per cent. Furthermore, adjustment for fiscal drag and slow growth of real incomes also affected tax proceeds in recent years. Consequently, the share of income taxes in total compensation of employees increased only little. For average incomes, it rose from 9.2 per cent in 1978 to 10.2 per cent in 1987.

49

As noted in Part I, the share of incorporated firms in the business sector is very small. Corporate profits have been taxed at rates somewhat lower than in Germany, but higher than, for example, in Belgium, Denmark, the Netherlands and in particular Switzerland. Corporate taxpayers have, however, benefited from favourable investment allowances and accelerated depreciation schemes, as well as investment tax credits. By deducting from corporate tax rates total tax allowances, it can be seen that the tax treatment of capital formation in the corporate sector is quite favourable by international comparison, with important subsidy elements involved, in

Diagram 11. **AVERAGE TAX WEDGES**[1]

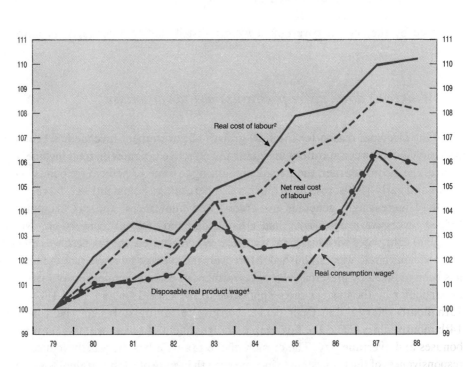

1. The average "tax wedge" is the difference between the average real cost of labour and the average real wage after: (i) social security contributions, (ii) direct taxes, and (iii) indirect taxes. All variables are deflated by a value added deflator, with 1979 = 100.
2. Total compensation per employee.
3. (2.) minus social security contributions.
4. (3.) minus direct taxes.
5. (4.) minus indirect taxes.
Source: OECD.

particular if it is debt-financed and if inflation is low (Annex II, Table 1). As shown by McKee *et al.* (McKee 1985) the total marginal tax rate on capital attributable to the corporate tax system as a percentage of the pre-tax rate of return, has been negative except for structures financed by new share issues or retained earnings. In recent years, the effective average rate of corporation tax has been about 35 per cent against a top marginal rate of 55 per cent. In addition, profits of incorporated as well as of unincorporated businesses are subject to a trade tax (Gewerbesteuer), which in recent years amounted to an average effective rate of 16½ per cent.

Another salient feature of the tax system has been the steady widening of the wedge between the effective cost of labour to firms and employees' real wages, net of all taxes and social-security contributions (Diagram 11). The main factor behind this growing gap has been the steady relative rise in employers' and employees' social-security contributions. Though demand and supply conditions in the labour market eventually determine what part will be borne by labour and by firms, labour is unlikely to have borne the full brunt of increases in employers' social security charges. Wage bargaining takes place within the long tradition of social consensus (see OECD 1988a, Part IV). Generally, employers may have refrained from passing on to workers the full rise in non-wage labour costs for fear of adverse effects on productivity. Given the openness of the Austrian economy, firms in the internationally-competing sectors have had little scope for passing higher costs on to prices. However, the resulting pressure on profits has been attenuated by a falling direct tax burden.

Rapid accumulation of government debt

Since the first oil shock, the growth of revenues has been insufficient to match the expansion of expenditure. The general government shifted from a net lender to a net borrower position in 1975. Following some trend improvement up to the second oil shock, a renewed deterioration took place between 1980 and 1987 (Diagram 12). The weakening financial position can be attributed mainly to three factors: *deliberate budget measures* to support economic activity, *automatic stabiliser* effects during the low-growth period of the 1980s and the ballooning of *interest payments* associated with the rapid accumulation of government debt. According to OECD estimates, over the period 1974 to 1981, negative short-run cyclical effects raised the public sector deficit by ¾ per cent of GDP, and almost twice as much in the years 1981 to 1987. Given large import leakages in small open economies like Austria, efforts to stimulate the economy through deficit-spending proved to be particularly costly in budgetary

51

Diagram 12. **GENERAL GOVERNMENT NET LENDING**
(Per cent of GDP)

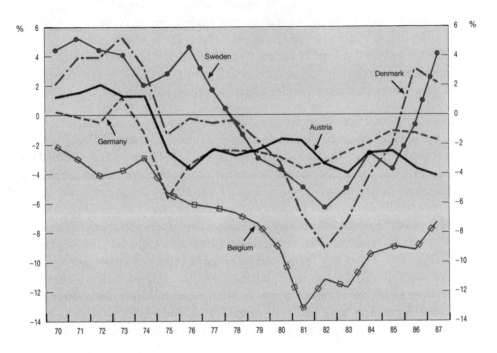

Source: OECD, *National Accounts.*

terms. Likewise, interest payments are generally providing little stimulus to demand, as they to a large extent serve to offset the erosion by inflation of the real value of financial assets.

Over the past decade, the sequence of deficits has led to a rapid build-up of public debt. General government gross indebtedness in relation to GDP passed the 50 per cent mark in 1987 compared to 30 per cent ten years earlier (Annex II, Table 2). Despite this rapid increase, the level of debt has remained below the OECD average and its rise over the past ten to fifteen years has been less marked than in most other smaller European countries. However, with the apparent interest rate on public debt being persistently higher than the rate of growth of nominal income, the trend rise in the debt to GDP ratio has as yet not been arrested (see below). Having no direct access to central bank finance, the Government covers financial deficits mainly

52

by long-term borrowing in domestic and foreign capital markets. Foreign indebtedness as a share of total federal government debt increased throughout the 1960s and 1970s, peaking at 32 per cent in 1981. Since then, its share has been almost halved. The banking system, not facing any placement restrictions, is the most important investor in government bonds. In the 1980s, it took up 80 per cent of net government debt issue.

The need to reduce government borrowing

As noted in Part I, the Government's aim to reduce the net federal deficit to 2½ per cent of GDP by 1992 is ambitious when seen against the earlier trend of rapid deterioration, but necessary if a spiralling of the debt/GDP ratio is to be avoided. Apart from the question of sustainability of persistently high levels of government borrowing, a rapid rise in indebtedness may also have adverse consequences for the longer-term growth potential of the economy through crowding-out effects on "productive" private investment. The rise in government borrowing in the 1980s has led to an increasing absorption of private sector savings (Table 16). To the extent that this has tended to put upward pressure on long-term interest rates, interest-rate-sensitive private expenditure would have been affected.

Table 16. **General government deficit and private sector savings**

	1977-82	1983-88	1986	1987	1988
		Annual average			
1. Private sector savings (Sch. bill.)	37.9	48.3	48.4	62.3	44.7
2. General government deficit (Sch. bill.)	23.0	47.9	52.2	61.2	42.7
Ratio (2 :1)∗100	60.7	99.2	107.9	98.2	95.5
Share of foreign borrowing in federal government deficit financing	0.35	0.05	0.07	0	..

Sources : Österreichische Postsparkasse, *Finanzschuldenbericht 1988*, and OECD.

It is, however, difficult to asses the importance of such crowding-out effects. There are no quantitative credit controls; external finance for productive investment is mainly provided by the banking system. Moreover, given the high degree of capital market exposure and the official objective of exchange rate stability, domestic interest rates are above all governed by foreign rates. Even so, the evolution of public finance may influence interest rates in two ways: through non-monetary deficit-financing, requiring higher interest rates for portfolio diversification reasons, or through a fiscal-policy-induced deterioration of the current external balance, requiring high interest rates for exchange rate reasons. Such interest rate effects could be attenuated in the short term by recourse to monetary financing or borrowing abroad, though, in the longer run, this may create financial instability. From 1978 to 1982, foreign capital markets were, indeed, heavily tapped, such borrowing accounting for half of the total increase in federal indebtedness. To the extent that such borrowing was not sterilised in the money market, this meant monetisation of debt. In the subsequent period, from 1983 to 1987, foreign borrowing was much less important, falling to about 5 per cent of new net debt. The sharply increased federal financing needs in the 1985 to 1987 period coincided with a surge in household saving, enabling the authorities to place a greater part of the new debt on the domestic capital market.

The increase of the structural budget deficit (the general government financial balance adjusted for cyclical influences) in the 1980s does not appear to have directly influenced the course of real interest rates (Diagram 13). Following its rebound from the inflation-induced slump in the early 1970s, the long-term real interest rate peaked in the post-OPEC II recession in 1981. Its subsequent modest tendency to decline coincided with a widening of the structural deficit. However, as elsewhere, the real long-term interest rate has remained above the rate of growth of real output; were this feature to persist, it would be bound to have negative implications for growth of investment and employment.

In assessing the need to reduce public sector borrowing, the budgetary implications of continuing debt accumulation are important. The general government deficit more than doubled from 1¾ per cent of GDP at the beginning of the 1980s to close to 4½ per cent in 1987. Assuming a 5 per cent rate of growth of nominal income over time, the maintenance of a deficit of this magnitude would imply a rise in the gross debt/GDP ratio from 50 per cent in 1987 to an ultimate "steady state" level of 90 per cent. An immediate reduction of the deficit to 2½ per cent of GDP would have been required to keep the debt/GDP ratio at its present level of 50 per cent. However, the relation between nominal income growth and the level of interest rates also has important bearings on the composition of government spending and, ultimately, on the sustainability of government borrowing itself. From 1980 to 1987, the apparent interest rate on debt – interest payments in relation to gross outstanding debt – rose

54

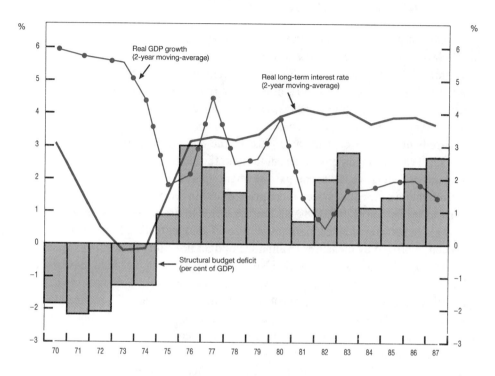

Sources: OECD, *National Accounts* and *Financial Statistics*.

marginally from 6.7 per cent to 6.9 per cent. As the debt/GDP ratio reaches its steady-state level, the burden of interest payments would have risen from 3½ to 6¼ per cent of GDP. Hence, keeping the overall budget deficit at 4½ per cent of GDP would require the *primary deficit*, the deficit before interest payments, to move into surplus to the tune of 1¾ per cent of GDP. Moreover, the timing of spending reductions influences the size of the eventual cuts in outlays necessary to reach given targets. The smaller the spending cuts in the initial phase of the programme, the faster the growth of debt and interest payments, hence the greater the need for spending restraint in the future to generate the required primary surplus.

The policy response

Expenditure restraint

Against the background of these trends, it became increasingly clear towards the mid-1980s that measures of expenditure restraint had to be taken. The brunt of the restraint fell in the first place on general government consumption and investment. Since the beginning of the 1980s, outlays for the provision of public services have declined as a share of total outlays, from 50 per cent to 40 per cent. Government employment growth has been scaled back to an annual rate of just 1 per cent compared with 3½ per cent in the 1970s. In the federal area, employment actually shrank in 1988. Government wages, notably in the central administration, have been losing ground relative to earnings elsewhere in the economy. The reduction of government investment has been more pronounced in recent years, reflecting in part a return to levels before the 1982-83 employment programmes were launched, and partly also a transfer of investment projects to off-budget bodies. Expenditure control has been improved by measures to enhance budget flexibility and transparency. The earmarking of receipts for specific spending areas such as road construction, telecommunications and promotion of residential construction has been partly discontinued. The financing burden of the federal railways has been reduced through cuts in personnel and overtime, and less generous tariff rebates, while budget control has been strengthened by a more efficient accounting system. Finally, the nationalised industries have been subject to a major restructuring process so that federal transfers should no longer be required once financial support programmes related to past commitments peter out (see Part I).

Since the mid-1970s, a series of small-step reforms have been implemented to contain the rapid rise in federal contributions to social security. The 1985 reform entailed a change in the method of calculating the pension-adjustment index reducing it by 0.1 percentage point for each percentage point of unemployment. At the same time, the assessment period was increased by 5 years for new pensioners and in the event of early retirement. In the 1988 reform, the assessment period for early retirement was further lengthened, while, generally, contribution-free years related to higher education were only partially taken into account. These reforms have ensured a better balance between pension benefits, contributions and income during working life. These two reforms and other measures are estimated to reduce federal subsidies to the pension system by an accumulated amount of some Sch. 200 billion between 1978 and 1995, with the larger part of the savings accruing in the latter part of this period. For 1989, savings may, however, reach Sch. 17 billion corresponding to

56

a quarter of federal transfers to the pension fund. As to the pensions of civil servants (amounting to Sch. 62 billion in 1987) there was no reduction of benefits but an increase of contributions.

The 1989 tax reform

The main principles

The difficulties experienced in curbing government current expenditure growth raises the question about the scope for enhancing revenue growth. In July 1988, the Coalition Government introduced the most comprehensive tax reform since World War II, taking effect from January 1989. Its central elements are the new personal income and business tax systems (Table 17). In addition, a number of other tax laws have been streamlined and adjusted (for details, see Annex I). While the main objective has been to achieve a simplification of the income tax system, a reduction in marginal rates and a more transparent distribution of the tax burden, the elimination and reduction of special allowances and tax credits should help increase tax responsiveness and revenue growth over time. Though designed to be broadly revenue-neutral over the longer term, the reform is not likely to be so within the time horizon the Government has given itself to achieve its goal for the budget deficit.

For *personal income taxation*, the top marginal rate has been lowered from 62 per cent to 50 per cent and the bottom rate from 21 per cent to 10 per cent, reducing significantly progressiveness (Diagram 14). At the same time, the number of tax brackets has been reduced from ten to five, and tax credits have been scaled back. Moreover, the tax base has been broadened by curtailing tax allowances and exemptions. However, preferential treatment of the 13th and 14th month salary has been maintained. As a net result of these changes, the average statutory tax rate on personal incomes has been lowered between 4½ and 6½ percentage points for taxable income of under Sch. 200 000, and the gap between (statutory) marginal rates and average rates of taxation has been narrowed. The majority of households whose tax base will be increased by less than 25 per cent through cuts in tax reliefs, will benefit from the reduction in tax rates. About 90 per cent of taxpayers will pay less taxes and an estimated additional number of 220 000 income-earners (or about 15 per cent more than earlier) will not pay income taxes at all. Comparing average taxation for real income brackets in 1989 with those of 1982, the year of the last inflation-adjustment of tax brackets, shows significant declines for all income groups (Table 18).

Table 17. **Major changes in taxation**

	Previous law	Present law (1989)
Personal taxes		
Tax rates	10-rate brackets from 21 to 62 per cent	5-rate brackets from 10 to 50 per cent
Tax allowances[1]		
Tax-free income		
Employees	Sch. 6 800 per month	Sch. 8 500 per month
Self-employed	Sch. 43 000 per year	Sch. 57 000 per year
Lump-sum deduction for expenses	Sch. 4 914	Sch. 1 800, minimum
Tax credits		
General tax credit	Sch. 6 460 to Sch. 8 460	Sch. 5 000
Wage-earner's tax credit	Sch. 4 000	Sch. 5 500
Single earner's tax credit	Sch. 3 900 plus Sch. 600 per child (maximum yearly income of Sch. 10 000)	Sch. 4 000 plus Sch. 1 800 per child (maximum yearly income of Sch. 20 000 for couple without children and Sch. 40 000 for couple with children)
Capital gains tax	20 per cent rate applicable to income from shares and certain kinds of bonds	25 per cent rate for those capital gains taxed at 20 per cent before
		Introduced at a 10 per cent rate for savings deposits and fixed interest-rate bonds
Trade taxe for unincorporated business	4 rates : from 5 per cent to 8 per cent Tax-free allowance : Sch. 80 000	2 rates : 4½ per cent and 6 per cent Tax-free allowance doubled
Corporate taxes		
Taxe rates	Four rates from 30 per cent to 55 per cent	30 per cent single rate
Trade tax	5 per cent	4½ per cent, proportional
Investment reserve allowance	25 per cent	10 per cent (since 1988)
Accelerated depreciation allowance	40 per cent for equipment investment	–

1. Central government.
Sources : Ministry of Finance, *Wirtschaftsbericht, 1988* and W. Nolz, P. Quantschnigg, *Österreichs Steuerreform*, Vienna 1988.

With respect to *corporate taxes*, the earlier progressivity of taxation has been eliminated: the three top marginal rates (at 55, 50 and 40 per cent) have been dropped, with the 30 per cent bottom rate becoming the standard rate. At the same time, the *trade tax* (Gewerbesteuer) on all business profits has been reduced by a tenth to around 15 per cent, while the tax-free allowance for self-employed and unincorporated firms has been doubled. As in the case of personal income taxation, the lowering of tax rates has been accompanied by a widening of the tax base. The accelerated depreciation of equipment investment has been abolished and the

Diagram 14. **REFORM OF PERSONAL TAXATION**

Statutory marginal rates

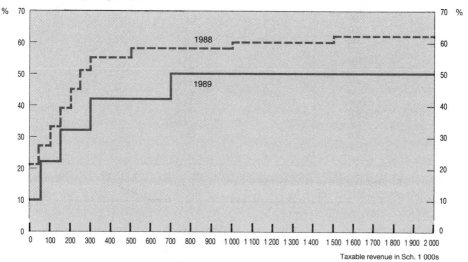

Taxable revenue in Sch. 1 000s

Difference between statutory marginal and average rates

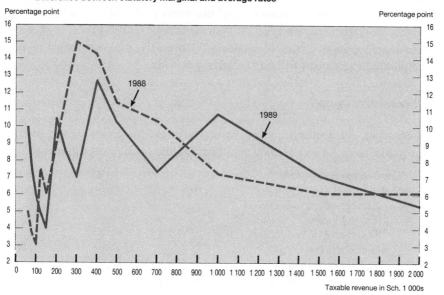

Taxable revenue in Sch. 1 000s

Source: WIFO (1988).

59

Table 18.   **Taxation of comparable real incomes in 1982 and 1989**

Income[1]	Average tax rate[2]		
	1982	1989	Reduction in per cent
50	0	0	0
100	1.1	0	–100.0
150	6.4	3.1	–51.5
200	8.6	6.4	–25.9
250	11.1	8.9	–19.7
300	13.2	11.6	–12.5
350	15.4	13.3	–13.3
400	17.5	14.7	–16.3
450	20.2	16.6	–17.7
500	22.6	18.9	–16.1
600	26.5	22.4	–15.6
700	29.7	24.8	–16.5
800	32.1	26.7	–17.1
1 000	35.9	29.8	–17.1
1 500	41.6	35.7	–14.3

1. Gross yearly average income of a married employee with one child, thousand schillings.
2. In per cent of gross yearly average income.
Source :   Ministry of Finance.

standard investment allowance has been lowered from 25 to 10 per cent. As shown in Diagram 15, incorporated companies at high level of profits (above Sch. 0.6 billion), will benefit most from the new taxation system, as their total tax rate, at 38 per cent, is lower than for unincorporated business. Conversely, at lower levels of profits, unincorporated enterprises will pay relatively less tax.

The budget impact

According to official estimates, the first year *net budgetary impact* of the tax reform would be as follows (billion schilling, middle of the range figures):

Gross revenue shortfall		45
less		
Savings on tax reliefs	28	
Capital income	3¾	
Shortening of tax-collection lags	2	
Indirect taxes	1¼	
Net revenue shortfall (before revenue sharing)		10

The tax base for personal incomes should widen by about Sch. 90 billion, generating additional tax receipts of Sch. 28 billion. The extension of the capital income tax

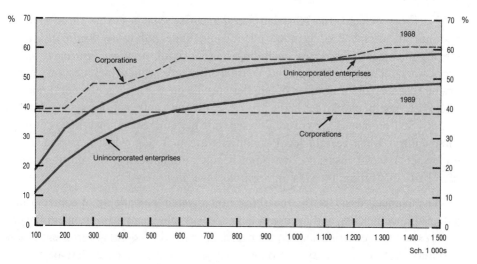

Diagram 15. **REFORM OF BUSINESS TAXATION**
Per cent of profits

Source: WIFO (1988).

should yield additional Sch. 3½ billion and the rate increase about Sch.¼ billion. In this context, it should be noted that measures taken in 1987 and 1988, such as the withdrawal of investment premia and of marriage benefits, provided additional revenues of Sch. 5 billion. The full positive impact of the tax reform will only be felt over the medium to longer-run. However, *uncertainties* necessarily attach to these estimates. While it is notoriously difficult to evaluate the impact of cuts in tax reliefs on the tax base, much will also depend on induced demand and, in particular, supply-side effects which are equally difficult to assess.

Financing social security: growing deficits ahead

The uncertainties attaching to future revenue trends have accentuated concerns about the growth dynamics of transfer payments, underlining the need for tighter expenditure control over the medium- to long-run. In particular, widespread fears have been voiced that the growing deficits of the social security system constitute a potential "time bomb", undermining efforts to consolidate the financial position of the public sector.

Narrowly defined, the Austrian social security system covers three areas of insurance, all administered by independent bodies under public law: *health insurance*, covering all medical expenses, including hospital care; *accident insurance*, which covers work-related accidents; and *pension insurance*, which includes two major pension schemes and a number of smaller specific ones. There is a general pension system catering for employees in the private sector and a state pension system for civil servants. Self-employed are covered by separate systems. Social insurance coverage is mandatory: when certain legal conditions are met (e.g. when a person enters employment) social insurance coverage begins automatically. In addition, under federal administration, there is an *unemployment insurance* fund.

The financial basis for the social insurance system is made up of contributions from insurance holders, and in case of dependent employment, also from employers. To the extent that contributions do not match benefits, the federal government covers the difference. Social security fees are levied as a per cent of earnings, but are subject to ceilings (Table 19). In 1988 the total ceiling became effective at monthly incomes of Sch. 27 600. The contribution for employees was 15.4 to 16 per cent, and for employers between 19.2 and 22.6 per cent. Two-thirds of contributions go to pension insurance. In the event of unemployment, the federal government takes over the payment of contributions. Social security contributions have grown steadily over time, attaining in 1987 a level corresponding to 13.6 per cent of GDP. Only in Belgium, France and the Netherlands, are contributions relatively higher.

Table 19. **Social security contribution rates**
Per cent of gross wages

	Blue-collar workers			White-collar workers		
	Total	Employees	Employers	Total	Employees	Employers
Health insurance	6.3	3.15	3.15	5.0	2.5	2.5
Accident insurance	1.4	–	1.4	1.4	–	1.4
Pension insurance	22.8	10.25	12.55	22.8	10.25	12.55
Unemployment insurance	5.2	2.6	2.6	5.2	2.6	2.6
Other	2.9	–	2.9	0.1	–	0.1
Total	38.6	16.0	22.6	34.5	15.35	19.15

Source : Hauptverband der Österreichischen Sozialversicherungsträger, *Übersicht, 1988.*

Benefits from social security schemes are only partially contribution-related. Unemployment benefits are calculated on the basis of previous earnings. In 1987, average unemployment insurance payments were almost 50 per cent lower than average incomes from employment, making the aggregate replacement ratio close to the European average. As to pensions, the initial amount is determined by the acquired pension rights, being in turn a function of contributions and length of working life. Pension payments, adjusted yearly on the basis of average wage developments, are subject to taxation. For workers with average pension rights, the old-age pensions amount to 80 to 85 per cent of disposable pre-pension income levels for men and 65 per cent for women. Pensions have on average increased faster than the gross compensation per employee, raising the relative benefit level from 0.43 in 1961 to 0.53 in 1987.

In 1987, total costs of social welfare, broadly defined, amounted to Sch. 412 billion or almost 28 per cent in terms of GDP. Apart from outlays of the social security system itself (Sch. 225.7 billion net of inter-scheme transfers), this includes government social expenditure as well as some occupational, and not legally-regulated, social services. Over time, calls on federal resources for social security transfers have grown, oscillating since 1978 between 26 and 28 per cent of total government outlays (including outlays for government pensions) (Table 20). Individuals' and employers' general contributions covered only some 80 per cent of total outlays of the social security system, the major part of the deficit originating in the pension system (Table 21). The federal contribution to pension payments accounts for 10 per cent of total federal outlays. The federal share covers 22 per cent of the

Table 20. **Share of social security transfers in government outlays**
Per cent of total outlays

	Unemployment insurance	Family benefits	Pensions (civil servants)	Pension insurance	Total
1978	1.6	10.0	7.6	8.3	27.4
1979	1.7	9.8	7.6	8.1	27.2
1980	1.8	9.5	7.5	7.0	25.9
1981	2.1	9.3	7.4	7.0	25.8
1982	2.7	9.1	7.4	8.1	27.3
1983	3.0	8.4	7.1	9.6	28.1
1984	3.0	7.7	7.1	9.6	27.1
1985	3.0	7.5	7.1	9.0	26.8
1986	3.1	7.2	7.0	9.0	26.3
1987	3.4	7.5	7.2	10.0	28.1

Source: Österreichisches Institut für Wirtschaftsforschung, Soziale Sicherheit 1987, in *Monatsberichte*, 7/1988.

Table 21. **Social insurance schemes : outlays and contributions**[1]

Schilling billion

	1984	1985	1986	1987
1. Health				
Outlays	50.7	53.3	56.7	60.4
Contributions	45.6	47.6	50.4	53.8
Other receipts	–	–	6.0	6.6
Balance	–5.1	–5.7	–0.3	0
2. Accident				
Outlays	7.6	8.3	8.9	9.5
Contributions	7.4	7.7	8.2	8.4
Other receipts	–	–	0.4	0.4
Balance	–0.2	–0.5	–0.3	–0.7
3. Pension				
Outlays	139.3	148.5	158.1	168.6
Contributions	99.2	107.4	112.8	117.1
Other receipts	–	–	1.9	0.9
Balance	–40.1	–41.1	–43.4	–50.6
4. Central government contribution to social insurances (1+2+3)	45.4	47.3	44.0	51.3

1. Excluding inter-scheme transfers.
Source : Ministry of Social Affairs, *Bericht über die soziale Lage 1987*.

employees pension benefits, two-thirds of civil servants' pensions, 69 per cent for insured self-employed, and three-fourths in the case of farmers' pensions. The following paragraphs discuss the likely emergence of larger deficits in the pension system as a result of medium- to long-term demographic changes, and consider options available to the federal government to reduce calls on its resources in the future.

The pension issue: the background

Total pension expenditure has increased much faster than nominal income and general government outlays, a feature shared with most other OECD countries (Diagram 16). Between 1960 and 1987, pension payments expressed in terms of GDP rose from 9½ per cent to 15 per cent, i.e. to the highest level in the OECD area. The rise was most pronounced in the years after the first oil shock, reflecting a marked rise in the number of beneficiaries and lower real growth rates (Annex II, Table 3). During the fifteen-year period to 1985, rising pension expenditure accounted for

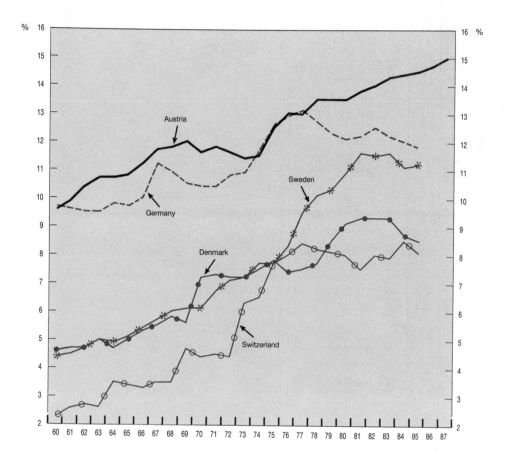

Diagram 16. **PENSION EXPENDITURE**
(Per cent of GDP)

Source: OECD (1988 b).

more than a quarter of the increase in the public sector share in GDP, and not far short of half in the first half of the 1980s (Annex II, Table 4).

Pension payments are determined by the number of beneficiaries and the amount each pensioner receives. Table 22 provides an international overview of the contribution of these two components to the growth of pension expenditure in the three sub-systems: old age, invalidity and survivors pensions. While the number of

65

Table 22.   **Components of pension expenditure growth, 1960-1985**

Annual percentage growth rates

	All pension benefits			Old age			Invalidity			Survivors		
	Deflated expenditure	Benefi-ciaries	Real benefits/capita	Deflated expenditure	Benefi-ciaries	Real benefits/capita	Deflated expenditure	Benefi-ciaries	Real benefits/capita	Deflated expenditure	Benefi-ciaries	Real benefits/capita
Austria (1960-85)	7.27	2.28	4.88	8.39	3.27	4.96	5.21	1.44	3.71	7.39	2.02	5.26
Belgium (1971-83)[1]	8.07	2.97	4.95	7.48	2.96	4.39	8.70	4.13	4.40	6.56	2.46	3.99
Denmark (1960-83)[2]	5.22	2.10	3.05	4.81	1.52	3.24	6.87	3.47	3.29	4.23	2.97	1.23
Germany (1960-85)	5.48	2.71	2.70	6.34	3.87	2.38	4.06	2.18	1.84	5.30	2.24	2.69
Netherlands (1960-85)[3]	8.33	4.29	3.87	7.20	2.96	4.12	9.82	6.74	2.89	5.30	1.81	3.43
Sweden (1960-84)	7.70	2.87	4.69	7.28	2.80	4.35	8.97	3.43	5.36	10.02	4.68	5.10
Switzerland (1960-84)	9.07	2.13	6.80	8.94	1.95	6.89	13.88	7.34	6.10	6.08	0.19	5.88
Average OECD area[4]	7.80	3.42	4.23	7.72	3.31	4.29	8.16	4.12	3.89	7.12	3.28	3.49

Note: The change in deflated expenditure is divided into two components, the change in the number of beneficiaries and that in real benefits per capita.
1.   Old-age, survivors : 1971-84.
2.   Invalidity, survivors : 1960-82.
3.   Invalidity : 1965-85.
4.   Geometric mean excluding France, Portugal, Iceland and Turkey.
Source :   OECD 1988b.

beneficiaries expanded less fast in Austria than on average in the OECD area, real benefit levels per pension receiver have increased significantly faster than on average, except for invalidity pensions.

Looking more closely at pensions, which constitute by far the largest proportion (70 per cent) of total social insurance expenditure, a more detailed breakdown of causal factors behind pension expenditure growth is provided in Table 23 and in Annex II, Table 5. In Austria, as in most other countries, changes in the eligibility ratio and the transfer ratio have been most important. This is hardly surprising, given that social insurance schemes have been extended to new groups and pension levels have been raised relative to real disposable wage income. Moreover, benefits are positively correlated with the duration of employment and as the system matures, a growing number of people is entitled to the highest benefits in each income category. The ageing of the population (the dependency ratio) and the lowering of the average pension age (inactive ratio) have also contributed to the rise of the pension expenditure ratio. By international comparison, Austria almost tops the list of countries with the highest contribution from the eligibility ratio; it moderately exceeds the average as far as the impact from the inactive ratio is concerned and there has been less-than-average pressure from the ageing of the population. The transfer ratio has made a very important contribution but only fractionally more than on average elsewhere.

Table 23. **Breakdown of the change in the expenditure ratio for old-age pensions, 1960-1985**
Ratio of end-year to initial-year values

	Change in expenditure ratio	Due to changes in :			
		Dependency ratio	Eligibility ratio	Transfer ratio	Inactive ratio
Austria	3.03	1.14	1.78	1.36	1.09
Belgium (1971-84)	2.10	0.95	1.42	1.39	1.12
Germany	2.10	1.32	1.72	0.78	1.18
Netherlands	2.28	1.20	1.22	1.34	1.16
Switzerland (1960-84)	3.53	1.31	0.97	2.58	1.07
Average of OECD countries[1]	2.46	1.26	1.41	1.35	1.03
Contribution to change (per cent)	–	25.6	38.0	33.2	3.2

Note : The dependency ratio is the ratio of the population aged 65 or more divided by the active population aged between 15 and 64 years. The eligibility ratio is the ratio of the actual number of pensioners to the population in the age group of 65 years or more. The transfer ratio is the average level of pensions. The inactive ratio is the inverse of the participation rate for the age group of 65 years or more.
1. Geometric mean, excluding Belgium, France, Portugal and Spain.
2. Total pensions.
Source : See Annex II, Table 5.

The problem of an ageing population

As noted above, the pension reforms of 1985 and 1988 have attenuated short-term financing difficulties of the pension insurance, but have not yet fully tackled the impending long-term ageing problem of the population, encapsulated in Diagrams 17 and 18. The former diagram shows the aged-dependency ratio in selected countries as calculated by the OECD (OECD 1988). Official estimates (Ministry of Social Affairs 1988) suggest that by the year 2030, the number of people aged 60 and over (rather than aged 65 and over as in Diagram 17) will have increased

Diagram 17.   **OLD-AGE POPULATION RATIO
IN SELECTED OECD COUNTRIES[1]**

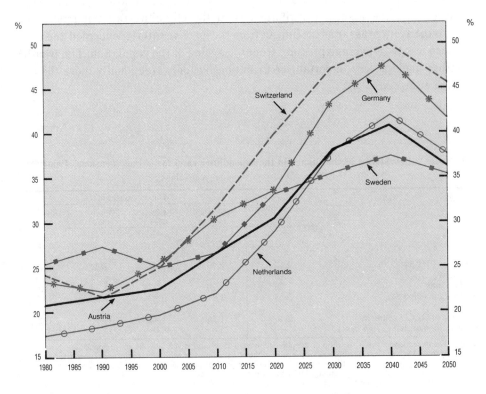

1.   [Population 65+/population 15-64] × 100; 1980 actual ratios; 1990 to 2050 projected ratios.
Source: OECD (1988 b).

Diagram 18. **AGE PROFILE OF PER CAPITA SOCIAL EXPENDITURE**

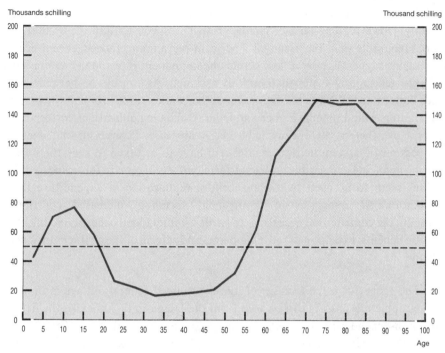

Thousands schilling

Thousand schilling

Age

Source: P. Findl and al. (1987).

by about 700 000 or some 50 per cent. As a result, their share in the total population will have gone from about 20 per cent to more than 30 per cent, raising the aged-dependency ratio from 32.5 per cent in 1986 to 56 per cent in 2030. Given the age profile of social expenditure, as calculated by Findl *et al.* (Findl *et al.* 1987) the consequences for government outlays are clearly worrying (Diagram 18). Under present pension payment rules and at unchanged contribution rates, federal transfers to the pension scheme would reach some Sch. 80 billion by 1995, and hence increase the federal financing share from 30 per cent in 1987 to 33 per cent in 1995.

Projections of future pension burdens are, of course, quite sensitive to underlying assumptions. In the above calculations, real income per capita of the active population is seen to grow by 1¾ per cent until the year 2000 and by 1½ per cent thereafter. The rate of unemployment is projected to increase by ¼ of a percentage point per year, reaching 7½ per cent of the dependent labour force by the mid-1990s. On this basis, the number of contributors to the pension system would decline steadily. However, long-term economic growth prospects until the year 2000 may be more favourable than the assumed 2 per cent per annum. Indeed, recent economic projections suggest a more or less stable unemployment rate and per capita incomes are expected to grow faster than initially assumed. As a result, higher participation rates, lower unemployment or bigger inflows of workers from abroad, the number of contributors would then be higher and federal financing obligations correspondingly lower. Nevertheless, there seems to be a large measure of consensus that, even under less pessimistic assumptions, measures will have to be taken to keep the burden of pension financing compatible with long-term budget targets. In this respect, different options seem to be open to the authorities: reallocation of expenditure between age-determined categories of government spending, increased contributions, changing the contribution bases, e.g. towards a value-added concept, modification of pension benefits, extension of retirement age, and reform of the civil servants' pension scheme.

The scope for a *reallocation* of age-determined federal outlays is limited for demographic reasons. As can be seen from the Diagram in Annex II, the decline in the youth-dependency ratio occurs in the years up to the end of the 1980s, while the rise in the old-age dependency ratio takes place thereafter. This means that the potential for savings on youth-related expenditure will diminish when the shifting age-distribution starts making itself felt on pension outlays. Even so, simple model calculations suggest that if it were possible to reallocate in full savings in youth-related expenditure, the federal share of social expenditure in terms of GDP would be 10 percentage points lower than otherwise.

A study (Busch 1988), completed prior to the 1988 reform, considers the implications of different demographic scenarios for *contribution rates* necessary to finance future pension expenditure (Diagram 19). In the central projection (Diagram 19), the pension levy would have to rise to more than 10 percentage points above the present level. Allowing this to occur would result in a full shifting of the burden of a rising dependency ratio onto future workers, in the sense that the net incomes of the latter would fall relative to that of pensioners. Conversely, if some of the burden of population ageing is to be shared by future workers and retirees, *pension levels* relative to wages would have to be reduced. In the central projection, the required cut works out at 30 per cent over the next 25 years. Allowing for the effects

Diagram 19. **IMPLICIT CONTRIBUTION RATES TO COVER FUTURE PENSION BURDENS**[1]

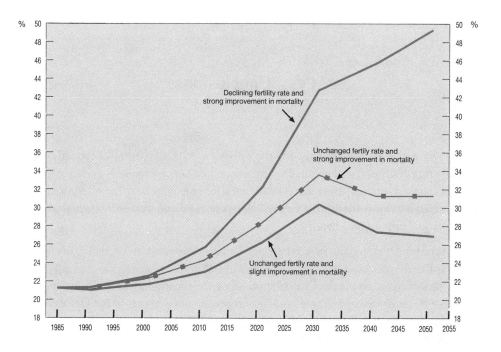

1. Unchanged/declining fertility rate are estimated at 1 per cent/0.7 per cent from 1991; strong/slight improvement in mortality implies an increase in life expectancy of 8.5/4 years by 2051.
Source: Busch (1988).

of the 1988 reform would reduce somewhat the required contribution rates in future years without altering the main findings of the study.

Another possibility to relieve the transfer burden for future active generations would be to *extend retirement age*. At present, the legal pension age is 65 for men and 60 for women. The actual retirement age is, however, closer to 60 and 55, respectively, given widespread use of early retirement schemes. Available model calculations show that a one-year prolongation of working life would at the present age structure reduce pension outlays by Sch. 2¼ billion, or some 1½ per cent of current pension expenditure. The net effect for total social expenditure would be smaller to the extent that unemployment increases.

71

IV.   Conclusions

1988 has been a good year for the Austrian economy: total output grew at a healthy rate of around 4 per cent; employment picked up, increasing by more than the labour force for the first time since 1979; inflation, measured by the rise in the GDP deflator, came down further to below 2 per cent; and the current external account remained in broad equilibrium.

A number of partly non-recurrent factors contributed to these favourable results. Firstly, because of its export structure, Austria benefited at an early stage from the increased strength of world trade since the second half of 1987. Second, the remarkable resilience of financial and foreign-exchange markets to the October 1987 stock market crash had positive effects on business and consumer confidence. Third, clement weather conditions early in the year boosted building and related activities, and finally, the speedy and early voting of the 1989 Tax Reform, apart from inducing business to advance investment projects, seems also to have had a confidence-building effect.

Given the much-improved business climate in Austria and her major trading partner countries, the outlook for the coming year or two remains satisfactory, though, with less favourable shifts in the structure of demand and less idle capacity, the growth of output may recede into the range of 2 to 3 per cent per annum. Exports should remain the most dynamic growth component. With monetary policy continuing to be accommodating and the cyclically-adjusted budget deficit projected to rise slightly in 1989, the expansion of private domestic demand can also be expected to hold up relatively well, in particular in the event of a further drop of the personal saving ratio as assumed in the OECD projection. On these trends and with productivity growth likely to remain strong, employment growth might only be moderate, permitting little further reduction in unemployment. However, strong productivity growth in conjunction with projected wage developments and mainten-ance of a stable schilling/Deutschemark relation should keep inflationary pressures at bay. With no further terms-of-trade gains expected, the current external balance is unlikely to change much over the projection period.

During its first two years in office the present Government has implemented two important reform projects: a major income tax reform and a comprehensive restructuring of nationalised industries, including partial privatisation with majority share holdings, however, being maintained by the public sector. At the same time, steps were taken to reverse the previous trend deterioration in the Federal financial position. Positive supply-side effects can be expected to arise from each of these initiatives. First encouraging results are already apparent but it will take a few more years before the full impact can be assessed.

The restructuring of the state-owned holding company, ÖIAG, has been nearly completed. The production capacity and the labour force in structurally-weak sectors, such as steel, have been further slimmed. Management independence has been strengthened and the most apparent operating inefficiencies have been removed. Thanks to a better conjuncture, the ÖIAG is now expected to break even in its current operations two years earlier than according to initial plans. To create greater financial room for manœuvre, sizeable asset sales have been made over the past two years and further selling is envisaged in coming years. However, except for a few smaller firms, the authorities have maintained a majority holding in all state-owned enterprises. In order to fully exploit potential efficiency gains, it is important that these firms are subjected to the same financial discipline and regulatory conditions as competing privately-owned enterprises; and, equally important, that markets in which these enterprises operate are, or are made, competitive.

The tax reform, voted in Parliament in mid-1988 and introduced at the beginning of 1989, is the most comprehensive since 1945. The original objectives, laid down in the Coalition Working Agreement of December 1986, of making taxation – both with regard to personal and business income – fairer and simpler have been met by lowering marginal tax rates and broadening the tax base. Marginal tax rates have been lowered relative to average rates. Even so, the response of income tax revenue to nominal income growth should become more favourable than in the past during which the tax base had been progressively eroded. By reducing allowances and exemptions and by closing tax loopholes and legal tax shelters, transparency of the tax system has been improved. The differential between the top personal income rate and the uniform corporate tax rate should *prima facie* tend to strengthen the move towards incorporation of firms. A number of fiscal particularities have, however, survived the screening process of the income tax system, of which the preferential tax treatment of the 13th and 14th month salary and of retirement-related lump-sum payments are the most prominent examples.

73

Faced with a rapid trend deterioration of its financial position, reflected in rising deficits, debt/GDP ratios and interest payments, the Government at the start of the present legislature established a medium-term budget consolidation programme aimed at cutting the net financial deficit from about 5 per cent of GDP in 1986 to 2½ per cent by 1992. Looking at budget outcomes in 1987 and 1988 on an administrative basis, it would seem that the Government is broadly on track thanks to appreciable expenditure restraint exercised on public consumption and investment. However, in limiting the net borrowing requirement to 4.7 per cent of GDP in 1987 and to an estimated 4.2 per cent in 1988, the Government was greatly aided by the unexpected strength of the economy. In assessing the sustainability of factors behind the budget consolidation process it should also be borne in mind that there are limits to further investment cutbacks and continued asset sales. The tax reform will not facilitate matters over the next few years. While designed to be revenue-neutral over the medium run, it will entail revenue losses in 1989 and the early 1990s. The first-year shortfall of Sch. 10 billion, of which about half is carried by the Federal government, will, however, be more than offset by a stepping-up of asset sales and a transfer of built-up reserves from 1988. Thus, the envisaged further cut of the federal budget deficit to 4 per cent of GDP in 1989 is greatly dependent upon non-recurrent sources of finance. Keeping the budget consolidation process on track to meet the medium-term objective set for 1992 will probably therefore require further significant measures of restraint.

Looking beyond the current legislative period, there are a number of positive as well as negative aspects which will have a bearing on public finance. On the positive side, there is a distinct possibility of supply-side effects resulting from the tax reform to raise the growth potential of the Austrian economy, especially if accompanied by further measures of deregulation and subsidy limitation. Subsidies to the business sector, though not particularly high by international comparison, are pervasive, comprising a wide range of schemes. Moreover, major areas of the economy, both in goods and services sectors, are subject to detailed regulation, reducing competition and the dynamism of the economy at large. As noted in Part I of the Survey, a number of positive steps have been taken in these two areas, but the scope for further moves to ease supply constraints and enhance economic efficiency has remained large. The budget balance should eventually also benefit from the recent and prospective progress in putting the nationalised sector of the economy on a sounder footing, enabling public enterprises to get external finance in the capital market on equal terms with private companies. For some more years to come, the Federal budget will, however, still be burdened with losses incurred in state-owned enterprises in previous years. On the negative side there is above all the continued rise in transfer payments and the obligation of the Federal government to cover the associated growing deficits of the social security system.

Apart from unemployment benefits, the rapid rise in social expenditure has been mainly due to steadily increasing pension outlays, in turn a combination of several factors: a growing tendency towards early retirement; extension of eligibility for social security coverage; a rise in average pension levels relative to wages due to a progressive maturing of the pension system and deliberate policy actions to raise benefit levels. In addition, the financial burden on the Federal government has been exacerbated by a narrowing of the contribution base entailed by a continuing shift of employment towards the public sector and, since the early 1980s, the rise in unemployment. The steady increase in social-security contribution rates, which are now among the highest in the OECD area, has by itself been insufficient to check the rise in federal transfers to the pension insurance system. The pension reform measures taken in 1985 and in 1988 have attenuated the long-term problem rather than solved it.

The already-existing problems of partially funding contribution-related pensions out of general tax revenue will be further aggravated by the ageing of the population. The available options for social security finance are a matter of simple arithmetic, involving price and/or quality adjustments. On plausible assumptions as regards fertility rates and life-expectancy, the implicit old-age contribution rate required to meet all pension obligations in the event of no change to pension entitlements would have to rise by about 50 per cent over the next four decades. At the other extreme, keeping contribution rates unchanged and freezing government transfers to the old-age pension system at present real levels, average pensions relative to compensation of employees would have to decline by more than a third. In the absence of any adjustment of contribution rates and benefit entitlements, federal transfers to the old-age pension insurance would have to double in real terms. Numerous combinations exist within these three solutions. There are, of course, also other measures which could be taken to ease the financing problem, e.g. prolongation of working life; full dependence of pensions on peoples' life-time income and contributions; widening of the social security tax base; harmonisation of benefit levels of different pension schemes. Immigration could also affect the picture. The package of measures eventually to be chosen will obviously be a political question. None of the various solutions can clearly be favoured on *a priori* grounds, although a simultaneous easing and equitable sharing of future transfer burdens between the active and the inactive part of the population would seem to be the most reasonable outcome. In addition, to make up for any reductions in public pensions, future pensioners could be encouraged to participate more actively in the prior formation of wealth, including claims on private insurance.

Summing up, the Austrian economic performance has been much better than expected a year ago. A favourable international environment has played a vital role. Progress has been made in many areas of policy, as regards both microeconomic reform and reduction of macroeconomic imbalances. But more needs to be done. The Government has reached its mid-term, and it is important to keep up momentum in efforts to improve supply conditions for output and employment. The dividend from sustained growth would greatly facilitate the task of budget consolidation and help solve the inter-generational transfer problem arising from the ageing population.

Notes and references

Busch, Georg (1988), "Auswirkungen der Demographischen Entwicklung auf einige Aufgabenbereiche der Öffentlichen Hand" in *Bevölkerungsrückgang und Wirtschaft"*, (Chaloupek G., J. Lamel and J. Richter, eds.), Vienna.

Federal Press Service (1987), *Agreement between the Socialist Party of Austria and the Austrian People's Party on the Formation of a Joint Federal Government for the Duration of the 17th Legislative Term of the Nationalrat*, Vienna.

Findl, Peter, Robert Holzmann and Rainer Münz (1987), *Bevölkerung und Sozialstaat*, Manzsche Verlags- und Universitätsbuchhandlung, Vienna.

McKee, M., J. Visser and P. Saunders (1986) "Marginal tax rates on the use of labour and capital in OECD countries", *OECD Economic Studies*, No 7, Autumn.

Ministry of Finance (1988), *Möglichkeiten des Einsatzes von Deregulierungsmassnahmen als wirtschaftspolitisches Instrument im Bereich des Gewerbes und der freien Berufe in Österreich*, Vienna.

Ministry of Social Affairs (1988), *Langfristige Finanzierung der Pensionsversicherung, Ergebnisse einer Arbeitsgruppe*, Vienna.

OECD (1988*a*), *Economic Survey of Austria*, February 1988.

OECD (1988*b*), *Reforming Public Pensions*.

WIFO (1988), Österreichisches Institut für Wirtschaftsforschung, "*Volkswirtschaftliche Effekte der Steuerreform*", Vienna.

Annex I

Calendar of main economic events

1987

January

New Banking Law takes effect. Main points were:

i) Rise in the capital ratio of banks to 4½ per cent of the *total* of all assets in the balance sheet

ii) New regulations to encourage risk capital.

The Austrian National Bank lowers its discount rate by ½ of a percentage point to 3½ per cent.

The interest rate on short-term open-market operations of the Austrian National Bank is put at 4½ per cent.

February

Banks lower the interest rates on savings deposits by ¼ to ½ of a percentage point to 3¼ per cent for the minimum rate on savings deposits and to 8¾ per cent for the prime rate.

Publication of expenditure plans for 1987 to be effective as of 1st April. The main point is that increases in VAT for a number of goods are dropped.

March

The voted federal Budget for 1987 projects a net deficit of Sch 74.7 billion (5 per cent of GDP).

June

The ceiling of full offsetting against tax of the purchase of new issues lowered to Sch 30 000 and to Sch 22 500 for participation certificates.

July

Banks lower the minimum interest rate on savings deposit by ⅝ of a percentage point to 2⅞ per cent, and the prime rate to 8¼ per cent.

The tax on land acquisition lowered from 8 per cent to 3.5 per cent.

December

Federal Budget for 1988 voted by Parliament. The budget deficit is projected at around Sch 71.1 billion, or 4½ per cent of GDP. Total revenues are expected to increase by 7½ per cent and expenditures by 5 per cent. Some tax concessions are suppressed (marriage allowance) or reduced (education allowance). Contribution rate to the unemployment funds increases by 0.8 percentage point to 5.2 per cent. Advanced depreciation facility for construction investment discarded as of end-December 1987.

The Austrian National Bank lowers its discount rate and the Lombard rate by ½ of a percentage point to 3 per cent and 4½ per cent, respectively.

1988

January

Banks lower the interest rates on savings deposits by ¼ to ½ of a percentage point to 8¼ per cent for the prime rate and to 2⅝ per cent for the minimum rate on savings deposits.

July

Tax reform voted by Parliament, to be enacted on 1st January, 1989. The main points are as follows:
- – Personal income tax brackets reduced to five with the top marginal tax rate lowered to 50 per cent and the bottom marginal tax rate to 10 per cent;
- – Corporation tax rate lowered to 30 per cent (single rate);
- – Trade tax rate lowered by 10 per cent;
- – Introduction of a withholding tax on interest income at a rate of 10 per cent;
- – Investment allowance reduced to 10 per cent;
- – Accelerated investment depreciation discarded;
- – A number of other fiscal allowances reduced or cut.

The rate of contribution to the public pension insurance to be increased by ½ of a percentage point to 9½ per cent as of 1st January, 1989.

The Austrian National Bank raises the Lombard rate by ½ of a percentage point to 5 per cent. The discount rate remains unchanged at 3½ per cent.

August

Banks raise interest rates on savings deposits by ¼ to ½ of a percentage point to 8¾ per cent for the prime rate and to 2⅞ per cent for the minimum rate on savings deposits.

The Austrian National Bank raises its discount rate by ½ of a percentage point to 4 per cent. The Lombard rate remains unchanged at 5 per cent.

December

The Austrian National Bank raises its Lombard rate by ½ of a percentage point to 5½ per cent.

1989

January

The Austrian National Bank raises the discount rate and the Lombard rate by ½ of a percentage point to 4½ per cent and 6 per cent, respectively.

Annex II

Supporting statistical material

Annex II Table 1. **Total marginal tax rate on capital attributable to the corporate tax system**

Per cent of pre-tax rate of return

	Zero inflation						Average inflation					
	Equipment			Structures			Equipment			Structures		
	Debt	New share issues	Retained earnings	Debt	New share issues	Retained earnings	Debt	New share issues	Retained earnings	Debt	New share issues	Retained earnings
Austria	-77.0	-14.7	-24.1	-18.2	23.8	17.5	-96.7	-15.9	-30.4	-49.3	17.0	5.2
Belgium	-100.3	-42.1	-37.7	-42.7	-1.3	1.9	-146.6	-51.5	-44.2	-87.2	-9.4	-3.4
Denmark	-19.6	3.3	-75.4	-8.5	12.2	-59.2	-53.1	-6.0	-177.0	-51.6	-4.8	-174.8
Germany	-39.2	-20.9	26.6	4.6	17.2	49.7	-76.8	-47.2	29.4	-49.0	-23.1	44.0
Netherlands	-76.4	-3.4	-124.5	-23.1	24.3	-56.7	-101.6	15.2	-174.6	-63.3	35.1	-125.9
Switzerland	-1.9	15.9	6.0	2.6	19.6	10.5	-7.3	19.1	0.8	-3.6	22.1	4.5

Note : These rates apply to returns to both households and tax-exempt institutions except in Sweden.
Source : McKee, *et al., OECD Economic Studies* No. 7, Autumn 1986.

82

Annex II Table 2. **General government gross indebtedness**

Percentage of nominal GNP/GDP

	1977	1978	1979	1980	1981	1982	1983	1984	1985	1986	1987	1988[1]
	Gross debt of general government											
Austria[2]	30.1	33.9	36.0	37.2	39.3	41.6	46.0	47.9	49.5	53.7	57.3	58.8
Belgium	63.4	67.6	71.5	77.4	89.3	97.0	106.9	112.2	118.6	121.4	125.2	127.9
Denmark[2]	18.1	21.9	27.0	33.5	43.6	53.0	62.6	67.0	65.3	59.2	57.2	54.8
Germany	28.5	29.9	30.7	32.5	36.3	39.5	40.9	41.5	42.2	42.4	43.3	44.0
Netherlands	39.7	40.9	42.7	45.9	50.3	55.6	61.9	66.1	69.6	74.3	80.4	84.5
Sweden	29.9	34.5	39.6	44.8	52.9	62.6	66.1	67.6	68.1	68.1	62.9	58.4
Total of smaller countries[3]	30.6	33.2	35.1	36.4	40.2	44.3	49.1	52.5	55.3	55.8	56.3	56.0
Total of European countries[3]	40.7	42.2	42.2	42.5	44.8	48.3	51.1	53.8	55.7	56.6	57.4	57.5
Total of above countries	39.6	40.8	40.6	41.6	42.9	46.7	50.0	51.8	54.3	55.9	56.3	56.0

1. Projection.
2. Partly estimated.
3. Does not exclude public sector mutual indebtedness.
Sources : OECD *National Accounts* and projections.

Annex II Table 3. **Expenditure elasticities of public pensions**

	1965-84/85	1965-74	1974-84/85	1974-79	1979-84/85
Austria	1.18	1.97	1.31	1.43	1.19
Belgium (1965-83)	–	–	1.47	1.49	1.41
Denmark	1.26	1.44	1.11	1.22	1.00
Germany	1.15	1.25	1.02	1.15	0.86
Netherlands	1.33	1.30	1.38	1.67	0.93
Switzerland	1.70	1.84	1.48	2.89	1.03
OECD average[1]	1.33	1.35	1.31	1.42	1.19

1. Unweighted geometric average, Belgium not included.
Sources : OECD *National Accounts* and Social Data Bank, Expenditure Section.

Annex II Table 4. Changes in expenditure shares[1]

	1960-1975			1975-1979			1979-1985		
	Total	Pension	Other	Total	Pension	Other	Total	Pension	Other
Austria	10.41	2.90	7.51	2.81	0.98	1.83	2.28	1.01	1.27
Belgium (1971-82)	. .	. .	. .	4.81	1.13	3.67	6.48	0.93	5.55
Denmark (1971-85)	. .	. .	. .	5.01	0.71	4.30	6.16	−0.01	6.17
Germany	16.52	2.93	13.58	−1.39	−0.34	−0.96	−0.19	−0.40	0.21
Netherlands (1970-85)	. .	. .	. .	3.02	1.90	1.12	4.13	−0.25	4.37
Switzerland	11.59	5.36	6.23	1.16	0.40	0.76	1.10	0.08	1.02
OECD average[2]	11.65	2.81	8.84	2.06	0.74	1.32	4.88	1.03	3.85
OECD average as a percentage of total change in each period	100.0	24.1	75.9	100.0	35.9	64.1	100.0	21.1	78.9

1. Expenditure as a percentage of GNP/GDP. The expenditure-share changes are calculated as final-year share minus initial-year share, expressed in percentage points. The first column is therefore the sum of the second and third columns.
2. Unweighted average.
Note : Total public expenditures mainly consist of current disbursements plus gross capital formation. It is the sum of the lines 38 (Outlay account), 9, 10, 13, 14 and 15 less line 2 and 3 (Capital accumulation account) in Table 6 of National Accounts Volume II, Detailed tables. Only current disbursements for Switzerland.
Sources : OECD, *National Accounts* and Social Data Bank, Expenditure section ; OECD, *Reforming Public Pensions*, Paris 1988.

Annex II Table 5.   **Breakdown of change in the expenditure ratio for old age pensions, 1960-1985**

Ratio of end-year to initial-year values

	Changes in expenditure ratio	Due to changes in :			
		Dependency ratio	Eligibility ratio	Transfer ratio	Inactive ratio
1. Insurance systems					
Austria	3.03	1.14	1.78	1.36	1.09
Belgium (1971-84)	2.10	0.95	1.42	1.39	1.12
Germany	2.10	1.32	1.72	0.78	1.18
France (1970-84)	1.57	0.95	*	*	1.11
Italy	2.92	1.39	1.57	1.13	1.17
Japan (1960-84)	7.53	1.54	2.99	1.56	1.05
Luxembourg[2]	1.57	1.18	1.64	0.82	0.99
Netherlands	2.28	1.20	1.22	1.34	1.16
Portugal (1960-84)	40.62	1.44	59.29	0.52	0.91
Spain (1974-85)	2.54	1.14	1.01	1.59	1.38
Switzerland (1960-84)	3.53	1.31	0.97	2.58	1.07
United Kingdom (1960-84)	2.28	1.15	1.55	1.40	0.91
Average[1]	2.82	1.27	1.60	1.29	1.07
Contribution to change (per cent)	–	23.7	45.6	24.7	6.6
2. Basic systems					
Australia (1961-85)	1.49	1.11	1.37	0.98	1.00
New Zealand	2.39	1.06	1.40	1.62	1.00
Average	1.89	1.08	1.38	1.26	1.00
Contribution to change (per cent)	–	12.2	51.1	36.7	0.0
3. Mixed systems					
Canada	2.33	1.18	1.57	1.43	0.88
Denmark (1960-84)	1.38	1.37	0.90	1.19	0.94
Finland (1960-84)	3.28	0.96	1.19	1.94	1.05
Ireland	2.33	0.96	1.19	1.61	1.26
Norway	2.61	1.42	1.45	1.55	0.82
Sweden	2.72	1.50	1.22	1.62	0.92
United Kingdom	1.75	1.28	1.23	1.04	1.07
Average	2.26	1.31	1.21	1.45	0.98
Contribution to change (per cent)	–	33.2	23.4	45.8	–2.40
Average of all the countries[1]	2.46	1.26	1.41	1.35	1.03
Contribution to change (per cent)	–	25.6	38.0	33.2	3.2

1. Geometric mean excluding Belgium, France, Portugal and Spain.
2. Total pensions.
Sources: OECD, *National Accounts, Labour Force Statistics* and Social Data Bank, Pension section.

85

Diagram. **YOUTH POPULATION RATIO
IN SELECTED OECD COUNTRIES**[1]

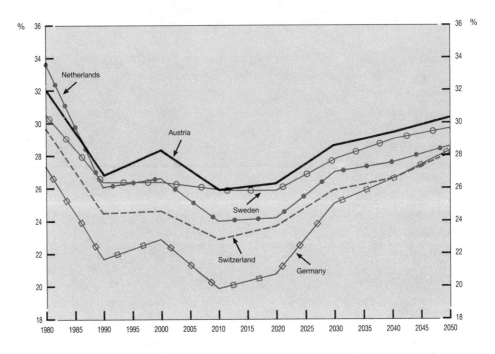

1.   [Population (0-14)/population 15-64] × 100; 1980 actual ratios; 1990 to 2050 projected ratios.
Source: OECD (1988 b).

86

STATISTICAL ANNEX

Table A. **Gross domestic product**
Sch. billion

	Current prices					1976 prices				
	1983	1984	1985	1986	1987	1983	1984	1985	1986	1987
Expenditure:										
Private consumption	694.8	733.2	775.0	803.3	830.1	484.5	483.2	493.7	501.7	513.8
Public consumption	226.9	237.8	255.0	271.0	281.0	155.2	156.1	159.7	162.3	163.4
Gross domestic fixed capital formation	267.7	281.0	302.0	319.6	334.1	184.3	188.7	198.0	205.2	209.0
Construction[1]	156.7	161.6	166.8	176.0	186.2	101.1	101.8	102.5	106.0	108.9
Machinery and equipment[1]	110.9	119.3	135.2	143.6	148.0	83.3	86.9	95.6	99.2	100.1
Change of stocks, incl. statistical errors	−3.9	22.9	13.8	16.0	24.5	1.7	17.4	15.6	22.7	29.8
Exports of goods and services	449.7	497.6	549.1	523.0	526.0	335.6	357.9	382.4	370.3	376.3
Less: Imports of goods and services	433.9	495.7	546.8	509.8	514.1	315.4	346.6	370.6	371.4	387.8
Gross domestic product at market prices	1 201.2	1 276.8	1 348.1	1 423.1	1 481.6	845.9	856.7	878.7	890.8	904.5
Origin by sector:										
Agriculture, forestry and fishing	44.1	48.7	45.0	47.5	48.6	41.6	42.9	40.9	41.5	41.7
Manufacturing and mining	328.1	345.6	368.8	389.1	396.8	251.7	258.0	267.1	271.2	270.4
Construction	87.4	87.1	89.1	93.4	99.6	54.5	53.4	54.0	54.7	55.8
Other	741.6	795.4	845.2	893.1	936.6	498.1	502.4	516.7	523.4	536.6

	Current prices					Current prices percentage distribution				
	1983	1984	1985	1986	1987	1983	1984	1985	1986	1987
Distribution of the national income:										
Compensation of employees	642.4	676.3	716.9	760.4	791.2	72.9	72.7	72.6	72.6	72.8
Income from property and entrepreneurship	247.5	265.6	280.8	302.4	317.7	28.1	28.6	28.5	28.9	29.2
Savings of corporations	19.8	21.9	25.1	25.7	25.0	2.2	2.4	2.5	2.5	2.3
Direct taxes on corporations	22.4	23.0	26.2	25.9	28.4	2.5	2.5	2.7	2.5	2.6
Government income from property and entrepreneurship										
Less: Interest on public debt and consumer debt	50.6	57.0	62.1	67.6	75.9	5.7	6.1	6.3	6.5	7.0
National income	881.5	929.8	986.9	1 046.8	1 086.4	100.0	100.0	100.0	100.0	100.0

1. Excluding VAT.
Sources: Österreichisches Statistisches Zentralamt, and Österreichisches Institut für Wirtschaftsforschung.

Table B. **General government income and expenditure**
Sch. billion

	1980	1981	1982	1983	1984	1985	1986	1987
Operating surplus and property income receivable	18.5	22.4	22.7	22.4	23.1	26.2	26.6	26.5
Casualty insurance claims receivable	0.2	0.2	0.2	0.2	0.2	0.2	0.3	0.3
Indirect taxes	162.8	174.4	185.0	197.1	216.1	225.9	234.0	243.8
Direct taxes	128.4	144.2	149.5	156.6	173.8	193.6	203.3	203.9
Compulsory fees, fines, and penalties	2.9	3.4	3.4	3.7	4.1	3.8	3.8	4.0
Social security contributions	124.6	133.4	139.8	145.5	155.5	167.8	175.9	183.0
Unfunded employee welfare contributions imputed	23.7	25.9	28.8	30.9	32.8	35.3	37.5	39.5
Current transfers n.e.c. received from the rest of the world	0.6	0.5	0.6	0.6	0.6	0.7	0.6	0.8
Current receipts	461.6	504.4	530.0	557.0	606.2	653.5	682.0	701.8
Final consumption expenditure	178.7	195.2	214.3	226.9	237.8	255.0	272.5	283.4
Property income payable	24.7	29.3	35.2	36.6	43.1	47.8	52.2	59.0
Net casualty insurance premiums payable	0.2	0.2	0.2	0.2	0.2	0.2	0.3	0.4
Subsidies	30.0	32.1	34.3	35.4	35.9	39.2	43.8	46.5
Social security benefits and social assistance grants	94.5	103.4	112.6	121.5	130.8	142.3	151.4	161.5
Current transfers to priv. non-profit inst. serving households	56.2	60.1	67.0	69.9	72.3	76.3	80.1	86.0
Unfunded employee welfare benefits	38.6	42.3	46.1	49.2	52.3	56.2	59.8	62.2
Current transfers n.e.c. paid to the rest of the world	2.5	2.7	3.0	3.2	3.5	3.7	3.8	3.9
Current disbursements	425.4	465.3	512.7	542.9	575.9	620.7	663.9	702.9
Saving	36.3	39.1	17.3	14.1	30.3	32.8	18.1	-1.1
Consumption of fixed capital	7.5	8.4	9.1	9.6	10.1	10.7	11.3	11.9
Capital transfers received, net, from	-16.5	-20.3	-20.0	-24.9	-25.2	-27.1	-27.9	-28.1
Other resident sectors	-16.4	-20.2	-19.9	-24.8	-25.2	-27.1	-27.9	-28.0
The rest of the world	-0.1	-0.1	-0.1	-0.1	0.0	0.0	0.0	-0.1
Finance of gross accumulation	27.3	27.2	6.4	-1.2	15.2	16.4	1.5	-17.3
Gross capital formation	41.6	43.8	42.9	45.2	46.3	48.0	50.4	50.9
Purchases of land, net	2.6	1.9	1.8	1.7	1.7	1.8	1.7	1.3
Net lending	-16.9	-18.5	-38.3	-48.1	-32.8	-33.4	-50.6	-69.5

Source: Bundesministerium für Finanzen.

Table C. **Output, employment, wages and productivity in industry**

	1984	1985	1986	1987	1987 Q1	Q2	Q3	Q4	1988 Q1	Q2	Q3
Output in industry, 1981 = 100, (adjusted for working days):											
Total industry[1]	105.4	110.3	111.6	112.1	107.0	115.9	104.5	119.2			
Mining and quarrying	102.9	101.9	98.7	101.9	101.9	107.5	94.0	105.2			
Investment goods	107.4	115.7	118.2	115.8	102.1	120.9	107.2	131.7			
Intermediate goods	114.3	120.8	118.5	122.9	117.5	129.9	112.2	130.8			
Finished goods	104.5	116.5	121.9	113.1	100.4	113.9	98.8	138.2			
Consumer goods	106.0	108.6	110.6	108.0	104.9	111.4	98.2	112.7			
Food, drinks, tobacco	104.0	107.8	109.6	107.8	98.6	105.5	99.1	109.7			
Durable goods	103.8	108.2	112.6	101.6	97.2	109.1	90.3	109.1			
Employment:											
Not seasonally adjusted ('000)[2]	561	562	559	544	545	543	547	540	531	530	536
Wages and productivity:											
Gross hourly earnings for wage earners (schillings)	90	95	99	104	91	111	96	119	94	115	99
Gross monthly earnings, employees (schillings)	18 626	19 755	20 713	21 505	18 548	22 839	19 858	24 774	19 399	23 811	20 510
Output per hour (1970 = 100)	208.2	217.6	225.6	235.2	214.9	237.2	237.4	251.3	234.6	255.8	262.5
Wages and salaries per unit of output (1970 = 100)	203.5	206.7	213.6	217.2	202.6	229.0	206.5	230.9	191.0	218.7	194.4

1. Figures for 1988 are not comparable to those earlier, and are not shown here.
2. Including administrative personnel.
Sources: Österreichisches Institut für Wirtschaftsforschung and Österreichisches Statistiches Zentralamt.

90

Table D. **Retail sales and prices**
(1985 = 100)

	1984	1985	1986	1987	1986 Q4	1987 Q1	Q2	Q3	Q4	1988 Q1	Q2	Q3
Retail sales:												
Total	95.5	100.0	100.7	103.6	115.4	89.5	101.2	101.2	122.5	98.2	106.8	105.2
Of which: Durables	90.5	100.0	108.0	113.0	123.3	90.3	115.8	113.7	132.4	111.7	129.3	117.5
Prices:												
Consumer prices												
Total	96.9	100.0	101.7	103.1	101.8	102.0	102.8	104.2	103.6	104.2	104.6	106.2
Food	97.8	100.0	102.4	103.2	102.4	102.8	103.7	103.4	102.8	103.2	104.1	104.3
Rent	95.0	100.0	103.2	106.5	104.6	105.5	105.9	107.1	107.6	108.1	108.6	109.2
Other goods and services	96.7	100.0	101.2	101.9	101.3	100.5	101.3	103.2	102.5	103.1	103.4	105.5
Wholesale prices												
Total	97.5	100.0	94.8	92.8	91.9	93.2	93.9	92.0	92.3	92.6	93.0	92.3
Agricultural goods	98.0	100.0	90.9	94.5	82.6	95.1	104.1	89.2	89.9	95.1	97.8	90.0
Food	96.7	100.0	100.1	97.4	99.1	98.3	97.2	97.1	96.8	96.7	96.7	96.4
Cost of construction (residential)	98.3	100.0	101.7	105.4	103.2	104.1	105.2	106.1	106.1	107.3	108.3	..

Sources: Österreichisches Statistisches Zentralamt, and Österreichisches Institut für Wirtschaftsforschung.

Table E. Money and banking[1]
End of period

	1985	1986	1987 Q1	1987 Q2	1987 Q3	1987 Q4	1988 Q1	1988 Q2	1988 Q3	1988 Q4
Interest rates (per cent):										
Discount rate	4.00	4.00	3.50	3.50	3.50	3.50	3.00	3.00	4.00	4.00
Average bond yield[2]	7.74	7.30	7.04	6.69	6.73	7.00	6.69	6.53	6.60	6.52
Money circulation and external reserves (Sch. bill.):										
Notes and coin in circulation	113.9	118.0	113.3	119.7	121.0	123.0	121.1	125.4	127.4	128.8
Sight liabilities of the Central Bank	46.6	53.0	43.2	46.5	46.8	43.6	43.9	47.6	48.9	39.6[4]
Gross external reserves of the Central Bank	110.5	115.0	112.5	114.3	113.5	114.9	126.1	125.3	128.8	123.4[4]
Of which: Gold	39.4	39.5	39.5	39.5	39.5	39.5	39.5	39.5	39.5	39.5[4]
Credit institutions (Sch. bill.):										
Credits to domestic non-banks	1 211.7	1 333.6	1 325.1	1 245.6	1 395.8	1 438.2	1 437.4	1 479.0	1 498.3	1 549.3[4]
Deposits from domestic non-banks	1 058.2	1 170.7	1 174.5	1 212.6	1 219.4	1 259.1	1 258.7	1 276.9	1 286.3	1 312.3[4]
Sight	107.5	113.5	108.0	122.9	125.5	129.1	123.4	138.8	138.7	142.3[4]
Time[3]	124.1	162.8	159.3	175.8	176.3	176.3	179.7	181.2	184.9	174.4[4]
Savings	826.6	894.4	907.2	913.9	917.6	953.7	955.6	956.9	962.7	995.7[4]
Holdings of domestic Treasury bills	41.0	41.0	42.0	47.0	48.1	51.2	54.6	56.3	54.8	46.9[4]
Holdings of other domestic securities	233.0	249.9	257.8	268.3	271.5	287.0	288.8	300.0	298.6	319.5[4]
Foreign assets	695.9	737.6	736.6	760.9	792.9	751.7	816.7	838.1	862.5	816.9[4]
Foreign liabilities	724.6	772.4	753.0	791.6	824.8	794.7	847.5	882.6	911.3	884.2[4]

1. Totals may not add due to rounding.
2. Average effective yields on circulating issues.
3. Including funded borrowing of banks.
4. Provisional data.

Sources: Österreichische Nationalbank and Österreichische Länderbank.

Table F. **The Federal budget**

National accounts basis
Sch. billion

		Outturn					
		1982	1983	1984	1985	1986	1987
1.	Current revenue	260.5	278.0	306.1	330.2	344.5	353.8
	Direct taxes of households	74.7	79.8	92.1	102.2	107.8	108.8
	Indirect taxes	130.5	139.7	151.5	157.9	164.4	170.9
	Corporate taxes	14.8	15.8	17.5	20.0	20.3	19.7
	Income from property and entrepreneurship	15.9	16.0	16.7	18.9	19.1	19.1
	Current transfers from abroad	0.3	0.3	0.3	0.4	0.3	0.6
	Other	24.3	26.4	28.0	30.8	32.6	34.7
2.	Current expenditure	275.3	300.0	316.2	340.3	365.6	383.0
	Goods and services	78.8	85.1	89.2	95.6	101.6	105.2
	Subsidies	26.1	27.4	27.8	30.0	34.1	36.9
	Public debt	25.3	27.0	33.8	38.4	42.7	47.4
	Transfers to abroad	0.9	0.9	1.0	1.0	1.0	1.1
	Transfers to public authorities	62.8	74.7	76.8	82.0	87.6	88.0
	Transfers to private households	52.8	54.6	55.5	59.1	62.2	66.2
	Other	28.6	30.3	32.1	34.2	36.4	38.2
3.	Net public savings (1 − 2)	−14.8	−22.0	−10.1	−10.1	−21.1	−29.2
4.	Depreciation	2.1	2.2	2.3	2.4	2.6	2.8
5.	Gross savings (3 + 4)	−12.7	−19.8	−7.8	−7.7	−18.5	−26.4
6.	Gross asset formation	14.1	17.0	18.0	17.8	18.1	18.5
7.	Balance of income effective transactions (5 − 6)	−26.8	−36.8	−25.8	−25.5	−36.6	−44.9
8.	Capital transfers (net)	16.4	22.9	22.5	23.7	25.2	26.1
9.	Financial balance (7 − 8)	−43.2	−59.7	−48.3	−49.2	−61.8	−71.0

Source: Österreichisches Statistisches Zentralamt.

Table G. **Balance of payments**

Sch. million

	1976	1977	1978	1979	1980	1981	1982	1983	1984	1985	1986	1987
Trade balance[1]	-52 516	-71 296	-50 675	-58 658	-87 483	-77 130	-62 613	-70 753	-76 784	-67 669	-62 231	-64 486
Exports	168 890	180 634	194 073	227 474	247 787	284 659	298 930	333 485	324 606	366 544	342 659	343 252
Imports	221 406	251 930	244 748	286 132	335 270	361 789	361 543	404 238	401 390	434 213	404 890	407 738
Services, net	28 053	24 414	30 466	34 855	42 159	41 393	46 158	40 434	48 430	49 085	42 007	38 559
Foreign travel, net	29 209	27 254	32 931	35 374	42 939	46 398	49 234	42 334	48 529	48 853	44 884	39 027
Receipts	56 437	61 958	68 551	75 010	83 363	90 952	95 031	94 386	101 026	105 186	106 195	96 116
Expenditure	27 228	34 704	35 620	39 636	40 424	44 554	45 797	52 052	52 497	56 333	61 311	57 089
Investment income, net	-3 847	-5 572	-7 071	-6 442	-6 838	-7 442	-6 962	-6 696	-7 029	-5 334	-10 103	-10 565
Other services, net	2 691	2 732	4 606	5 923	6 058	2 437	3 886	4 796	-7 128	5 566	7 226	10 097
Unclassified goods and services	7 472	13 921	11 129	9 319	25 093	15 692	29 877	35 777	25 626	18 045	24 631	24 906
Transfers, net	-1 910	-2 322	-130	387	-1 144	-1 363	-1 238	-1 456	-1 206	-1 947	-657	-77
Public	-194	-285	-160	-312	-399	-471	-608	-792	-766	-799	-690	-899
Private	-1 716	-2 037	30	699	-745	-892	-630	-664	-440	-1 148	33	822
Current balance	-18 901	-35 283	-9 210	-14 097	-21 375	-21 408	12 184	4 002	-3 934	-2 486	3 750	-1 098
Long-term capital, net	-1 261	9 828	20 430	-7 172	7 084	15 040	-9 864	-24 054	-7 097	-3 653	9 927	23 040
Official[2]	3 245	12 048	12 221	2 170	5 938	12 281	14 176	6 428	1 499	8 612	14 736	12 020
Private	-4 506	-2 220	8 209	-9 342	1 145	2 759	-24 040	-30 482	-8 596	-12 265	-3 792	11 020
Basic balance	-20 162	-25 455	11 220	-21 269	-14 291	-6 368	2 320	-20 052	-11 031	-6 139	13 677	21 942
Non-monetary short-term capital	-737	5 672	-371	-4 013	-5 210	2 004	-6 261	2 651	-4 199	2 166	-3 070	-7 784
Errors and omissions	2 587	1 147	3 084	1 013	2 865	4 508	10 623	-6 974	-2 080	11 626	-11 944	2 828
Balance on non-monetary transactions	-18 312	-18 636	13 933	-24 269	-16 636	144	6 682	-29 677	-17 310	7 653	-1 337	396
Private monetary institutions' short-term capital	14 997	11 628	3 227	7 256	38 313	7 984	-2 939	21 832	18 938	-8 854	9 788	-11 003

Changes in reserves arising from allocation of SDRs, monetization of gold and revaluation of reserve currencies											
−3 554	−2 160	9 278	7 935	4 413	3 974	803	6 519	4 706	−9 601	−6 960	−4 834
Allocation of SDRs											
0	0	0	598	560	597	0	0	0	0	0	0
Changes in total reserves											
−6 869	−9 168	26 438	−9 078	26 090	12 102	4 546	−1 326	6 334	−10 802	1 491	−92
Exchange rate (Sch. per dollar)											
17.94	16.53	14.52	13.37	12.94	15.92	17.06	17.97	20.01	20.69	15.27	12.64

1. Including non monetary gold and adjustments to trade according to foreign trade statistics.
2. Including Central Bank.
3. Excluding allocation of SDRs, monetization of gold and revaluation of reserve currencies.
Source: Österreichische Nationalbank.

Table H. Merchandise trade by commodity group and area

Sch. billion

	Imports					Exports				
	1983	1984	1985	1986	1987	1983	1984	1985	1986	1987
Total	348.3	392.1	431.0	408.0	411.9	277.1	314.5	354.0	342.5	342.4
By commodity group:										
Food, drink, tobacco	21.4	23.2	25.2	24.9	23.7	12.3	14.2	14.7	13.0	11.6
Raw materials	21.0	26.0	27.1	22.3	21.3	18.2	20.0	19.3	18.1	18.2
Mineral fuels, energy	48.1	59.2	64.1	35.4	29.8	3.9	4.8	7.3	4.3	6.2
Chemicals	35.0	39.3	43.0	41.1	42.4	25.9	30.6	32.3	29.6	30.8
Machinery and transport equipment	103.6	110.0	128.6	137.9	143.1	83.6	94.2	110.8	113.7	114.5
Other	119.2	134.4	143.0	146.4	151.6	133.2	150.7	169.8	163.8	161.1
By area:										
OECD countries	284.1	300.7	334.6	338.7	348.1	198.6	229.0	262.9	269.8	277.9
EEC countries[1]	218.4	236.9	263.1	272.9	280.1	148.8	167.8	192.0	205.8	217.0
Germany	144.6	156.5	176.4	179.5	181.9	85.3	93.1	106.6	112.1	119.3
Italy	30.9	33.8	35.5	36.5	38.7	24.6	29.5	31.8	31.8	35.5
France	14.3	14.5	15.6	16.0	16.7	10.4	12.2	14.0	14.7	15.3
UK	7.5	8.4	9.8	9.4	9.9	11.3	13.8	16.3	15.3	15.7
EFTA countries[2]	27.2	31.1	34.4	31.3	32.2	29.8	34.0	38.1	40.3	38.1
Switzerland	6.1	7.2	7.8	7.1	7.2	5.2	6.0	6.6	6.8	6.7
USA	11.7	13.7	16.0	13.1	14.2	8.2	12.9	16.5	13.8	12.2
Other OECD countries	26.8	19.0	37.1	21.4	21.6	11.8	14.3	16.3	9.9	10.6
Non-OECD countries										
COMECON Europe[3]	36.6	45.7	45.9	34.0	28.0	33.6	38.2	39.1	33.0	30.9
Africa[4]	11.7	16.6	18.9	11.1	9.1	11.4	12.3	13.2	8.6	7.3
Latin America[4]	8.0	8.1	9.8	7.3	5.6	2.9	3.4	3.8	3.6	3.2
OPEC	13.3	18.6	20.0	9.3	8.8	20.4	20.2	21.4	13.1	9.9
Far and Middle East[4]	13.9	16.1	16.8	12.6	16.7	23.1	23.3	25.5	19.3	15.7
Index, in real terms (1980 = 100)	101	109	116	120	127	111	122	134	134	138
Index of average value (1980 = 100)	109	114	119	107	102	111	114	116	112	109

1. From 1986, including Spain and Portugal.
2. Including Finland.
3. Excluding Yugoslavia.
4. Including countries belonging to OPEC.
Source: Österreichisches Institut für Wirtschaftsforschung.

BASIC STATISTICS :

INTERNATIONAL COMPARISONS

	Units	Reference period[1]	Australia	Austria
Population				
Total	Thousands	1987	16 249	7 575
Inhabitants per sq.km	Number		2	90
Net average annual increase over previous 10 years	%		1.4	0.0
Employment				
Total civilian employment (TCE)[2]	Thousands	1987	7 079	32 997
of which: Agriculture	% of TCE		5.8	8.6
Industry	% of TCE		26.6	37.7
Services	% of TCE		67.6	53.7
Gross domestic product (GDP)				
At current prices and current exchange rates	Billion US$	1987	193.7	117.2
Per capita	US$		11 919	15 470
At current prices using current PPP's[3]	Billion US$	1987	204.9	88.4
Per capita	US$		12 612	11 664
Average annual volume growth over previous 5 years . . .	%	1987	3.7	1.8
Gross fixed capital formation (GFCF)	% of GDP	1987	23.8	22.6
of which: Machinery and equipment	% of GDP		11.5 (86)	9.7
Residential construction	% of GDP		4.7 (86)	4.6 (86)
Average annual volume growth over previous 5 years . . .	%	1987	1.7	2.3
Gross saving ratio[4]	% of GDP	1987	20.3	24.1
General government				
Current expenditure on goods and services	% of GDP	1987	18.2	19.0
Current disbursements[5]	% of GDP	1987	35.0 (86)	46.6 (86)
Current receipts	% of GDP	1987	34.7 (86)	47.9 (86)
Net official development assistance	% of GNP	1987	0.33	0.17
Indicators of living standards				
Private consumption per capita using current PPP's[3] . . .	US$	1987	7 389	6 535
Passenger cars, per 1 000 inhabitants	Number	1985	. .	306 (81)
Telephones, per 1 000 inhabitants	Number	1985	540 (83)	460 (83)
Television sets, per 1 000 inhabitants	Number	1985	. .	300 (81)
Doctors, per 1 000 inhabitants	Number	1985	. .	1.7 (82)
Infant mortality per 1 000 live births	Number	1985	9.2 (84)	11.0
Wages and prices (average annual increase over previous 5 years)				
Wages (earnings or rates according to availability)	%	1987	5.7	4.9
Consumer prices	%	1987	7.0	3.0
Foreign trade				
Exports of goods, fob*	Million US$	1987	26 484	27 084
as % of GDP	%		13.6	23.0
average annual increase over previous 5 years	%		4.4	11.6
Imports of goods, cif*	Million US$	1987	26 964	32 580
as % of GDP	%		13.9	27.7
average annual increase over previous 5 years	%		2.8	10.8
Total official reserves[6]	Million SDR's	1987	6 441	6 049
As ratio of average monthly imports of goods	Ratio		3.4	2.6

* At current prices and exchange rates.
1. Unless otherwise stated.
2. According to the definitions used in OECD *Labour force Statistics*.
3. PPP's = Purchasing Power Parities.
4. Gross saving = Gross national disposable income *minus* Private and Government consumption.
5. Current disbursements = Current expenditure on goods and services *plus* current transfers and payments of property income.
6. Gold included in reserves is valued at 35 SDR's per ounce. End of year.
7. Including Luxembourg.
8. Included in Belgium.
9. Including non-residential construction.

EMPLOYMENT OPPORTUNITIES

Economics and Statistics Department, OECD

The Economics and Statistics Department of the OECD offers challenging and rewarding opportunities to economists interested in applied policy analysis in an international environment. The Department's concerns extend across the entire field of economic policy analysis, both macroeconomic and microeconomic, and it is also responsible for the collection, processing and dissemination of a wide range of internationally consistent statistics. On the economic side, its main task is to provide, for discussion by committees of senior officials from Member countries, documents and papers dealing with current policy concerns. Within this programme of work, three major responsibilities are :

- To prepare regular surveys of the economies of individual Member countries;
- To issue full twice-yearly reviews of the economic situation and prospects of the OECD countries in the context of world economic trends;
- To analyse specific policy issues in a medium-term context for the OECD as a whole, and to a lesser extent for the non-OECD countries.

The documents prepared for these purposes, together with much of the Department's other economic work and its statistical output, appear in published form in *OECD Economic Outlook*, *OECD Economic Surveys*, *OECD Economic Studies*, the Department's Working Paper series, and an extensive list of statistical publications.

The Department maintains a world econometric model, INTERLINK, which plays an important role in the preparation of the policy analyses and twice-yearly projections. The availability of extensive cross-country databases and good computer resources facilitates comparative empirical analysis, much of which is incorporated into the model.

The Department is made up of about 90 professional economists and statisticians from a variety of backgrounds from all Member countries. Most projects are done by small teams and last from four to eighteen months. Within the Department, ideas and points of view are widely discussed; there is a lively professional interchange; and all professional staff have the opportunity to contribute actively to the programme of work.

Skills ESD is looking for

a) Solid competence in using the tools of both microeconomic and macroeconomic theory to answer policy questions. In our experience, this requires the equivalent of a PhD in economics or substantial relevant professional experience to compensate for a lower degree.

b) Solid knowledge of economic statistics and quantitative methods; this includes how to identify data, estimate structural relationships, apply and interpret basic techniques of time series analysis, and test hypotheses. It is essential to be able to interpret results sensibly in an economic policy context.

c) A keen interest in and knowledge of policy issues, economic developments and their political/social contexts.

d) Interest and experience in analysing questions posed by policy-makers and presenting the results to them effectively and judiciously. Thus work experience in government agencies or policy research institutions is an advantage.

e) The ability to write clearly, effectively and to the point. The OECD is a bilingual organisation with French and English as the official languages. Candidates must have excellent knowledge of one of these languages and some knowledge of the other. Knowledge of other languages might also be an advantage for certain posts.

f) For some posts, expertise in a particular area may be important, but a successful candidate can expect to be asked to contribute in a broader range of topics relevant to the work of the Department. Thus, except in rare cases, the Department does not recruit narrow specialists.

g) The Department works on a tight time schedule and strict deadlines. Moreover, much of the work in the Department is carried out in small groups of economists. Thus, the ability to work with other economists, from a variety of professional backgrounds, and to produce work on time is important.

General Information

The salary for recruits depends on educational and professional back-ground, but positions carry a basic salary from FF 223 584 or FF 275 880 for Administrators (economists) and from FF 320 820 for Principal Administrators (senior economists). This may be supplemented by expatriation and/or family allowances depending on nationality, residence and family situation. Initial appointments are for a fixed term of two to three years.

Vacancies are open to candidates from OECD Member countries. The Organisation seeks to maintain an appropriate balance between female and male staff and among nationals from Member countries.

For further information on employment opportunities in the Economics and Statistics Department, contact :

Executive Assistant
Economics and Statistics Department
OECD
2, rue André-Pascal
75775 PARIS CEDEX 16
France

Applications citing "ECOU", together with a detailed curriculum vitæ in English or French, should be sent to:

Head of Personnel
OECD
2, rue André-Pascal
75775 PARIS CEDEX 16
France

WHERE TO OBTAIN OECD PUBLICATIONS
OÙ OBTENIR LES PUBLICATIONS DE L'OCDE

ARGENTINA - ARGENTINE
Carlos Hirsch S.R.L.,
Florida 165, 4º Piso,
(Galeria Guemes) 1333 Buenos Aires
Tel. 33.1787.2391 y 30.7122

AUSTRALIA - AUSTRALIE
D.A. Book (Aust.) Pty. Ltd.
11-13 Station Street (P.O. Box 163)
Mitcham, Vic. 3132   Tel. (03) 873 4411

AUSTRIA - AUTRICHE
OECD Publications and Information Centre,
4 Simrockstrasse,
5300 Bonn (Germany)   Tel. (0228) 21.60.45
Gerold & Co., Graben 31, Wien 1 Tel. 52.22.35

BELGIUM - BELGIQUE
Jean de Lannoy,
Avenue du Roi 202
B-1060 Bruxelles   Tel. (02) 538.51.69

CANADA
Renouf Publishing Company Ltd
1294 Algoma Road, Ottawa, Ont. K1B 3W8
Tel: (613) 741-4333
Stores:
61 rue Sparks St., Ottawa, Ont. K1P 5R1
Tel: (613) 238-8985
211 rue Yonge St., Toronto, Ont. M5B 1M4
Tel: (416) 363-3171
Federal Publications Inc.,
301-303 King St. W.,
Toronto, Ont. M5V 1J5   Tel. (416)581-1552
Les Éditions la Liberté inc.,
3020 Chemin Sainte-Foy,
Sainte-Foy, P.Q. GIX 3V6, Tel. (418)658-3763

DENMARK - DANEMARK
Munksgaard Export and Subscription Service
35, Nørre Søgade, DK-1370 København K
Tel. +45.1.12.85.70

FINLAND - FINLANDE
Akateeminen Kirjakauppa,
Keskuskatu 1, 00100 Helsinki 10 Tel. 0.12141

FRANCE
OCDE/OECD
Mail Orders/Commandes par correspondance :
2, rue André-Pascal,
75775 Paris Cedex 16   Tel. (1) 45.24.82.00
Bookshop/Librairie : 33, rue Octave-Feuillet
75016 Paris
Tel. (1) 45.24.81.67 or/ou (1) 45.24.81.81
Librairie de l'Université,
12a, rue Nazareth,
13602 Aix-en-Provence   Tel. 42.26.18.08

GERMANY - ALLEMAGNE
OECD Publications and Information Centre,
4 Simrockstrasse,
5300 Bonn   Tel. (0228) 21.60.45

GREECE - GRÈCE
Librairie Kauffmann,
28, rue du Stade, 105 64 Athens Tel. 322.21.60

HONG KONG
Government Information Services,
Publications (Sales) Office,
Information Services Department
No. 1, Battery Path, Central

ICELAND - ISLANDE
Snæbjörn Jónsson & Co., h.f.,
Hafnarstræti 4 & 9,
P.O.B. 1131 – Reykjavik
Tel. 13133/14281/11936

INDIA - INDE
Oxford Book and Stationery Co.,
Scindia House, New Delhi 110001
Tel. 331.5896/5308
17 Park St., Calcutta 700016   Tel. 240832

INDONESIA - INDONÉSIE
Pdii-Lipi, P.O. Box 3065/JKT.Jakarta
Tel. 583467

IRELAND - IRLANDE
TDC Publishers - Library Suppliers,
12 North Frederick Street, Dublin 1
Tel. 744835-749677

ITALY - ITALIE
Libreria Commissionaria Sansoni,
Via Benedetto Fortini 120/10,
Casella Post. 552
50125 Firenze   Tel. 055/645415
Via Bartolini 29, 20155 Milano   Tel. 365083
La diffusione delle pubblicazioni OCSE viene
assicurata dalle principali librerie ed anche da :
Editrice e Libreria Herder,
Piazza Montecitorio 120, 00186 Roma
Tel. 6794628
Libreria Hœpli,
Via Hœpli 5, 20121 Milano   Tel. 865446
Libreria Scientifica
Dott. Lucio de Biasio "Aeiou"
Via Meravigli 16, 20123 Milano   Tel. 807679

JAPAN - JAPON
OECD Publications and Information Centre,
Landic Akasaka Bldg., 2-3-4 Akasaka,
Minato-ku, Tokyo 107   Tel. 586.2016

KOREA - CORÉE
Kyobo Book Centre Co. Ltd.
P.O.Box: Kwang Hwa Moon 1658,
Seoul   Tel. (REP) 730.78.91

LEBANON - LIBAN
Documenta Scientifica/Redico,
Edison Building, Bliss St.,
P.O.B. 5641, Beirut   Tel. 354429-344425

**MALAYSIA/SINGAPORE -
MALAISIE/SINGAPOUR**
University of Malaya Co-operative Bookshop
Ltd.,
7 Lrg 51A/227A, Petaling Jaya
Malaysia   Tel. 7565000/7565425
Information Publications Pte Ltd
Pei-Fu Industrial Building,
24 New Industrial Road No. 02-06
Singapore 1953   Tel. 2831786, 2831798

NETHERLANDS - PAYS-BAS
SDU Uitgeverij
Christoffel Plantijnstraat 2
Postbus 20014
2500 EA's-Gravenhage   Tel. 070-789911
Voor bestellingen: Tel. 070-789880

NEW ZEALAND - NOUVELLE-ZÉLANDE
Government Printing Office Bookshops:
Auckland: Retail Bookshop, 25 Rutland Stseet,
Mail Orders, 85 Beach Road
Private Bag C.P.O.
Hamilton: Retail: Ward Street,
Mail Orders, P.O. Box 857
Wellington: Retail, Mulgrave Street, (Head
Office)
Cubacade World Trade Centre,
Mail Orders, Private Bag
Christchurch: Retail, 159 Hereford Street,
Mail Orders, Private Bag
Dunedin: Retail, Princes Street,
Mail Orders, P.O. Box 1104

NORWAY - NORVÈGE
Narvesen Info Center – NIC,
Bertrand Narvesens vei 2,
P.O.B. 6125 Etterstad, 0602 Oslo 6
Tel. (02) 67.83.10, (02) 68.40.20

PAKISTAN
Mirza Book Agency
65 Shahrah Quaid-E-Azam, Lahore 3 Tel. 66839

PHILIPPINES
I.J. Sagun Enterprises, Inc.
P.O. Box 4322 CPO Manila
Tel. 695-1946, 922-9495

PORTUGAL
Livraria Portugal, Rua do Carmo 70-74,
1117 Lisboa Codex   Tel. 360582/3

**SINGAPORE/MALAYSIA -
SINGAPOUR/MALAISIE**
See "Malaysia/Singapor". Voir
« Malaisie/Singapour »

SPAIN - ESPAGNE
Mundi-Prensa Libros, S.A.,
Castelló 37, Apartado 1223, Madrid-28001
Tel. 431.33.99
Libreria Bosch, Ronda Universidad 11,
Barcelona 7   Tel. 317.53.08/317.53.58

SWEDEN - SUÈDE
AB CE Fritzes Kungl. Hovbokhandel,
Box 16356, S 103 27 STH,
Regeringsgatan 12,
DS Stockholm   Tel. (08) 23.89.00
Subscription Agency/Abonnements:
Wennergren-Williams AB,
Box 30004, S104 25 Stockholm Tel. (08)54.12.00

SWITZERLAND - SUISSE
OECD Publications and Information Centre,
4 Simrockstrasse,
5300 Bonn (Germany)   Tel. (0228) 21.60.45
Librairie Payot,
6 rue Grenus, 1211 Genève 11
Tel. (022) 31.89.50
Maditec S.A.
Ch. des Palettes 4
1020 – Renens/Lausanne   Tel. (021) 635.08.65
United Nations Bookshop/Librairie des Nations-
Unies
Palais des Nations, 1211 – Geneva 10
Tel. 022-34-60-11 (ext. 48 72)

TAIWAN - FORMOSE
Good Faith Worldwide Int'l Co., Ltd.
9th floor, No. 118, Sec.2, Chung Hsiao E. Road
Taipei   Tel. 391.7396/391.7397

THAILAND - THAILANDE
Suksit Siam Co., Ltd., 1715 Rama IV Rd.,
Samyam Bangkok 5   Tel. 2511630
INDEX Book Promotion & Service Ltd.
59/6 Soi Lang Suan, Ploenchit Road
Patjumamwan, Bangkok 10500
Tel. 250-1919, 252-1066

TURKEY - TURQUIE
Kültur Yayinlari Is-Türk Ltd. Sti.
Atatürk Bulvari No: 191/Kat. 21
Kavaklidere/Ankara   Tel. 25.07.60
Dolmabahce Cad. No: 29
Besiktas/Istanbul   Tel. 160.71.88

UNITED KINGDOM - ROYAUME-UNI
H.M. Stationery Office,
Postal orders only: (01)873-8483
P.O.B. 276, London SW8 5DT
Telephone orders: (01) 873-9090, or
Personal callers:
49 High Holborn, London WC1V 6HB
Branches at: Belfast, Birmingham,
Bristol, Edinburgh, Manchester

UNITED STATES - ÉTATS-UNIS
OECD Publications and Information Centre,
2001 L Street, N.W., Suite 700,
Washington, D.C. 20036 - 4095
Tel. (202) 785.6323

VENEZUELA
Libreria del Este,
Avda F. Miranda 52, Aptdo. 60337,
Edificio Galipan, Caracas 106
Tel. 951.17.05/951.23.07/951.12.97

YUGOSLAVIA - YOUGOSLAVIE
Jugoslovenska Knjiga, Knez Mihajlova 2,
P.O.B. 36, Beograd   Tel. 621.992

Orders and inquiries from countries where
Distributors have not yet been appointed should be
sent to:
OECD, Publications Service, 2, rue André-Pascal,
75775 PARIS CEDEX 16.

Les commandes provenant de pays où l'OCDE n'a
pas encore désigné de distributeur doivent être
adressées à :
OCDE, Service des Publications. 2, rue André-
Pascal, 75775 PARIS CEDEX 16.

72380-1-1989

OECD PUBLICATIONS
2, rue André-Pascal
75775 PARIS CEDEX 16
No. 44681
(10 89 11 1) ISBN 92-64-13209-0
ISSN 0376-6438

•

PRINTED IN FRANCE